# Maggie Mamen, PhD

# WHO'S IN CHARGE?

## A Guide to Family Management

www.creativebound.com

P.O. Box 424
Carp, Ontario
Canada K0A 1L0
(613) 831-3641

ISBN 0-921165-47-1
Printed and bound in Canada

*This book is not intended to replace appropriate diagnosis and/or treatment, when indicated, by a qualified mental health professional or physician. Any names used as examples throughout this book have been changed to ensure privacy of individuals and families.*

Book design by Wendelina O'Keefe
Cover images © 1997 PhotoDisc Inc.

**Canadian Cataloguing in Publication Data**

Mamen, Maggie
    Who's in charge : a guide to family management

Includes bibliographical references.
ISBN 0-921165-47-1

    1. Parenting.  2. Family.  I. Title.

HQ769.M34  1997          649'.1          C97-900347-4

*Over the years I have developed a picture of what the human being living humanly is like. He is a person who understands, values and develops his body, finding it beautiful and useful; a person who is real and honest to and about himself and others; a person who is willing to take risks, to be creative, to manifest competence, to change when the situation calls for it, and to find ways to accommodate to what is new and different, keeping that part of the old that is still useful and discarding what is not.*

*When you add all this up, you have a physically healthy, mentally alert, feeling, loving, playful, authentic, creative, productive human being, one who can stand on his own two feet, who can love deeply and fight fairly and effectively, who can be on equally good terms with both his tenderness and his toughness, know the difference between them, and therefore struggle effectively to achieve his goals.*

*The family is the "factory" where this kind of person is made. You, the adults, are the peoplemakers.*

Virginia Satir
*Peoplemaking*

# Contents

# Acknowledgments

This book would not have been attempted, let alone finished, without the help and encouragement of a large number of people, many of whom are known to me only as faces in a crowd. All the parents who have attended my workshops, talks, seminars, groups and therapy sessions have supplied a richness of anecdotes and information that provide a daily learning experience — and have urged me to write this all down so that they could take it home and share it with the other half of the management team. Some of you will recognize yourselves and your children here. This has nothing whatsoever to do with the fact that names have been changed to protect the innocent, or that stories have been meshed and occasionally embellished. Rather it is due to the tremendous universality of experiences that exists despite enormous individual differences. Yes, I have been in your house and you have been in mine.

My daily learning experiences are also firmly rooted in the interactions I have with my circle of "consultants." Deep gratitude goes in particular to Sally Lees for her unconditional support and "therapy," Clare Bowles for getting me unstuck so many times and for all her insights, Sandra Wieland and Pen Deering for sharing their many different experiences of families, and to everyone at Centrepointe Professional Services where work becomes a second home and family.

**This whole project is dedicated, with love, to:**

*Rolf*, my partner for life, my co-manager and my friend, who teaches me that parenting is not a gender issue and that you do not have to shout (the former I have learned, the latter I am still learning);

*Natalie*, our first graduate, on whom we practised and who has turned out to be just fine, despite everything we did and tried to do;

*Katy*, who continuously prevents us from becoming complacent and who has taught us that different is not just okay, but exciting;

*Jorin*, our final trainee, who has benefited from the benign neglect and skepticism that comes with parental experience and who unashamedly reaps what his sisters have sown;

*Audrey*, my sister and co-trainee, whose courage has provided a rich ground for the seeds of many hours of thought and introspection;

and, last but not least, *Max*, our beloved dog, who gives us the reinforcement we need for our parenting skills when we most need it—and *never* talks back.

# Introduction

**1**

Laurie is brought in to my office by her parents, who tell me that their only daughter is not at all happy, and that they would like me to help them find ways to cheer her up and foster her self-esteem. They tell me that her happiness is PARAMOUNT to them and that they have tried absolutely everything to try to appease her. When I remark that she appears quite content to me (as children routinely do as they play in the office), they apologize profusely (just as all parents feel they must, in case I don't believe them) and assure me that she is The Child From Hell the rest of the time. With very little probing on my part, it becomes apparent that these parents are held hostage in their own house. Laurie doesn't let them go out to restaurants, to stores or to other people's houses. She demands their full attention all the time they are at home. She has specific ideas about what she will and will not eat, and does not hesitate to let them know when they do not guess correctly. She refuses to go to bed until she is good and ready—sometimes way past Mom and Dad's bedtime—and until she has had her full complement of stories, drinks, songs, back rubs, hangnail inspections, bathroom visits, lie-downs, and countless other ministries. And, they inform me, they **have** to give in to her every whim just to try to avoid the major rages and tantrums that result when they do not. They have long given up any thoughts of having other children—how could they ever manage with two or more when there are not enough hours in the day for one? Mom has even quit work because she thought that this would make Laurie happy. It hasn't.

Laurie is three years old. But she could be six, ten, fourteen or even twenty-one. The specifics may differ and the form of the tantrums may change, but the issue remains the same. This family has a Child in Charge. Laurie thinks she is management. When a child, however young or old, takes over as the head of the household, it is because parents have become powerless—for whatever reason—and the family starts to crumble. At such a point, it is time to reevaluate the entire hierarchy and for parents to take whatever steps are necessary in order to reinstate themselves in their jobs as Chairs, Presidents and Chief Executive Officers of the family.

Please don't get me wrong—I'm not blaming Laurie's parents. We have ALL been there. We have ALL had times when running the family has become a low priority because of fatigue, illness, preoccupation with other issues. We have ALL had children who tried for a takeover. And we shall ALL continue to revisit this situation, even after we have been enlightened over the next few chapters. This book provides an easy-to-follow model for family functioning, for troubleshooting to try to determine where things are going wrong when go wrong they will, for some basic ideas as to how to restore ourselves as parents to our rightful position as managers of the family, and most of all to reassure us all that this is where our children need us and where we need to be.

## The Job of Parenting

Parenting is the hardest job we are ever called upon to undertake—with little or no formal training, infinite hours on duty, no pay and no holidays. The responsibility of helping to shape the destiny of other human beings is awesome to most of us, and one that we do not undertake lightly; yet we find out very early on in the family management game that there are precious few people out there who are willing or able to help, or whose advice we gladly accept. No one else knows our children as we do, no one else is as invested in our family's well-being, and no one else's experiences exactly match our own.

The whole notion of parenting as a "job" was brought home to me at a time when I was juggling breast-feeding and second-year undergraduate child development study. For one of my courses, a workbook, aptly named "A Self-Directed Guide to the Study of Child Psychology" by a man named Gerard Levin, took great pains to outline the various qualifications for a wide range of jobs in the general field of childcare, ranging from community college to several postgraduate degrees, and encompassing such careers as teacher's aide, teacher, pediatrician, child psychologist, play nurse (don't ask, I have no idea), speech therapist, librarian, childcare worker, cottage parent in a residential institution… It was immediately and glaringly obvious to me that "parent" was missing from the list, and yet I was overwhelmed at that time by the competence I was clearly lacking, but was expected to have—both by society at large and by my tiny helpless infant—in all areas of childrearing and childcare. The author compounded my guilt and feelings of inadequacy by adding authoritatively:

"…the recent glorification of volunteers and amateurism has obscured the fact that in working with children there is no adequate substitute for technically sound professional training. Not even 'love' is enough. Watch a real 'pro' in action as a nursery school teacher or speech therapist if you don't believe it. As few as half a dozen specialized courses can make all of the difference between being a well-educated unemployment statistic and being a sought-after professional in an exciting and rewarding field."

Wow, and I thought all it took was a sperm, an egg, a moment of passion—and waiting for maternal instinct.

## The Myth of Maternal Instinct

The notion of maternal instinct has long struck me as a dangerous one. First and foremost, believing that women possess some "magical" powers of bonding to children that men somehow miss out on seems to cut out half the human race when it comes to implied competence at parenting. We have decades of research clearly showing that the young of the species will attach itself quite firmly to whichever caregiver happens to be the most accessible, provided that caregiver provides warmth and comfort—completely independently of whether that caregiver is equipped to provide food. Gender has never been an issue with this particular phenomenon. Parenting is not a gender issue. In fact, there are many men who are deeply attached to their children, and many women who are not. It would be of great benefit to society if more people understood the deep bond that men frequently have toward their children, and also if men were permitted by society (by other men, but primarily by women) to take more of an active role in early parenting. I have met many fathers who feel totally intimidated by the apparent competence of their wives to handle the children, and many of these same wives are totally burned out trying to parent alone, frequently because they believe they "should."

A second danger that arises from believing in maternal instinct is the guilt engendered in many mothers when they do NOT instinctively know how to respond to a child—when others are saying of the wailing infant, "he just wants his mom" or of the screaming toddler, "you'd better deal with him, you're his mom." Or, in fact, when instinct is telling us to panic, or to scream, or to shake a baby, or to flatten an obnoxious adolescent against a wall. I have now been waiting for more than 23 years for maternal instinct to kick in helpfully…and am still waiting.

If we can put aside the notion of *maternal* instinct and talk more about *parental* instinct, we open up the parenting business to both genders, and share the guilt more equitably. We can then accept more readily that parenting skills can be learned, rather than inherited, and make the job a truly shared responsibility.

## Other Myths of Parenting

You may be familiar with the folklore that some (often childless) people, including our own children, actively promote about parenting—the idea that children should be happy, that they have all kinds of equal rights, and that, out there somewhere, there is the ideal family with whom they are planning to run away and live.

**Happiness:**  While we all would like our children to develop into happy, well-adjusted human beings, it is clear that children spend a great deal of their childhood appearing to be quite miserable. Despite wanting to keep their children content, most parents can list the things it takes to keep the average 12-year-old happy—and realize the total impossibility of this goal, even in the short term. Happiness comes from learning to cope in the real world:  facing disappointments and coming through; making mistakes and learning from them; taking risks; making choices and experiencing the consequences of those choices; doing things independently and succeeding; overcoming obstacles by problem-solving; and from being nurtured and supported, even when things are not going well. When you grow up being given everything that you ask for as soon as you ask for it, or even when your parents avoid any situation that will make you unhappy, you internalize a set of messages about the world that do not in fact reflect the true situation. Accordingly, you fail to develop an adequate set of tools to help you deal with the disappointments, failures, mistakes and difficulties you will inevitably encounter. Spoiled children become spoiled adults who believe that the world "owes" them and who are perpetually disappointed and unhappy when their expectations are not met.

**Equality:**  Almost all children believe that they are not treated fairly, particularly in relation to their brothers, sisters and friends. We tend to believe that, in order to be "fair," it is necessary to treat our children equally—equal time, equal money, equal privileges, equal gifts, and so on. In fact, treating children of different ages equally backfires long before the oldest learns to drive. We acknowledge quite openly that each of our children is different (usually from the moment of conception) and we realize without too much introspection that we are in fact different parents to each of our children, because of their personalities, needs and attitudes. And yet the notion that we should treat them equally is a very persistent one. We agonize over the rivalries that build up between the children—each one vying for a little more attention, wanting to be first, demanding sovereignty—and yet we do not realize that we unwittingly set these up and support them by aiming for equality.

When a family who has a dog tries to introduce a second pup into the household, there are often a number of fights between the animals. Veterinarians will be the first to tell you that the way to reduce fights and jealousies in such a situation is to treat the older dog with the respect it deserves due to seniority alone, at least for the first while. They will tell you to ensure that the older dog knows that it has the more senior role; it gets fed first, petted first, talked to first, so that the other dog knows the hierarchy and so that the pecking order is clear. This approach will eliminate the unpleasant rivalries and restore a comfortable peace. Important to realize is that this has absolutely ***nothing*** to do with how much you love either dog, or how special each one is to you. Think about it. As humans we tend to do the opposite; we tend to introduce a new baby with the ultimate in pageantry and fanfare, and keep the older one waiting while we respond to the infant's every need, frequently continuing to blame an older sibling every time there is a scuffle or disagreement. To try to prevent rivalries or cries of "unfair!" we try to keep things equal. I would suggest to you that, when it comes to raising children, treating them equally is being ***un*fair.

**Everybody else's parents:** Our children, of course, all know that mythical family that lives "out there" somewhere. The parents in this family are perennially happy and benevolent. They never raise their voices. They would never dream of making their children wear snow pants, mitts, hats or boots in the winter; they allow them out at all hours of the day and night with their friends, never once wanting to know where they are, who they are with or what time they will be home; they provide all material goods and replace those that get broken, worn out or simply go out of style; bikes are allowed out with no helmets; teenagers are provided with cars; television, video games and movies are uncensored and freely available; and, most importantly for many children, homework is seen as a much lower priority than getting on with REAL LIFE issues. At some time or other, our children make efforts to go join this family. Five-year-olds pack bags and tell us they are leaving; 12-year-olds threaten constantly; 16-year-olds frequently try it out.

The problems arise when *we* start to believe that this family exists, and we back down on our expectations for our children or (worse still) change our value systems to try to be more in line with this family so we get a better report card from the children. While a reality check on our own expectations once in a while really doesn't hurt and can help us to make a few minor adjustments to keep up with the times, shifting value systems can provoke high levels of anxiety in children. They need to know what we expect of them so that they can relax and get on with the job of growing up healthy.

Fortunately, or unfortunately as the case may be, we are the only parents they have, however lousy we are at the job. We all do the best job we are able to do, given the information we have available to us and the skills we possess. What a scary thought.

**Rather than believe all the old myths, let us consider an alternative approach.**

What would happen if, for example, we assume that maternal instinct only exists in a favoured few and that the rest of us have to manage without? What if we recognize that love is not enough? What if we accept that children will not be happy at some of our parenting decisions and that if we wait for them to like everything, we shall all be six feet under, pushing up daisies? What if we acknowledge that seniority exists and that to treat all our children equally is in fact not being fair? And (horror of horrors) suppose we subscribe to the view that "Because I said so" is sometimes good enough?

**Above all, let's presume that parents are MADE, not BORN, that parenting is a job that can be learned, like any other, that there's no right or wrong way to do it, and that in fact you can run your family company any way you want.**

## From Dysfunctional to Functional

We hear and see too much in the media about "dysfunctional families"—the buzzwords of the 1980s and the 90s—with the result that parents feel blamed for a wide range of the world's problems. It seems that we cannot tell whether we have done a good job as parents until we find out whether our adult children and their families require therapy!

Over the years of working with a wide variety of families and simultaneously helping to raise children of my own, it has become clear to me that a model of "normal" family functioning is necessary if we are to find some guidelines by which to operate. Finding such a model in the popular literature without judgments as to what is "right" and "wrong" proves to be impossible, and many models of family therapy tend to look solely at communication patterns which are important, but in many cases are insufficient to deal with specific problems or crises that arise.

From the families that cross my office threshold on a daily basis, it has become painfully obvious that one of the main problems has been an imbalance within the family structure that results in the wrong individual being in charge, namely one or more of the children, while the parents are feeling powerless, anxious and angry.

## Characteristics of Children in Charge

We have already seen how Laurie could "run" her family by the age of three. While there may well be a myriad of individual differences among children even within the same family, there are *some* signals that can alert us to the fact that a child has taken over control in a family. Most of these behaviours are quite normal (with the possible exceptions of violence and damage to property)—in moderation, at certain ages, and if they are not used to manipulate or to cause deliberate harm. However, any one or several of these behaviours that persist, particularly if they result in parents "giving in" or "giving up," coupled with parental feelings of helplessness, would be sufficient to suspect a subtle or not-so-subtle "coup":

| | | |
|---|---|---|
| • **temper tantrums** | • **refusal to eat** | • **violence** |
| • **general defiance** | • **verbal abuse** | • **"shut-downs"** |
| • **increasing demands** | • **damage to property** | • **bossy behaviour** |
| • **bedtime conflict** | • **attention seeking** | • **babysitter problems** |

It is important to realize that a number of control behaviours are not easy to identify; you may have an easier time recognizing them in a child who is loud, extraverted, bossy and acting out, rather than in one who sulks, pouts, sobs inconsolably and shuts down.

 *Simon's Grade 4 teacher had first suggested he needed to see a psychologist because of difficulties he was having finishing his work in class. He seemed to be daydreaming a lot of the time, and even when he did have his mind on his work he worked at the pace of a disabled snail. When his teacher suggested that he should stay in at recess to finish his work, he cried quietly the whole time, so she had started to allow him to take home any work he had not completed and to do it for homework. Alison, Simon's mom, was at her wits' end at home. She was a single mom, having left a fairly abusive marriage three years previously, taking Simon and his younger brother Sam with her. The boys still saw their dad every second weekend, but he was pretty uninvolved otherwise, preferring to focus on his new partner and their baby daughter. Exchanges between Simon's parents were hostile at best, and frequently non-existent.*

*Alison reported that Simon seemed to be perpetually unhappy, from the time he arrived home from school until he eventually fell exhausted into bed. He and Sam seemed to be constantly fighting whenever they spent time together, and Simon was in fact almost at the point of bullying his brother—frequently trying to enlist Alison to "sentence" Sam to some dire punishment. In addition to acting as judge and jury, Alison was routinely spending two to three hours a night with Simon on his homework, during which time she had to stay constantly by his side because, whenever she tried to leave him to go help Sam, he would sit and do absolutely nothing. When she would try to make him do something, whether by threatening punishments, cajoling or nagging, he would variously burst into tears, stomp to his room and slam the door, yell like a banshee, or other variations on a similar theme. By about ten o'clock at night, both Simon and Alison would be totally drained (Sam had been sent off to bed with his teddy and his book), but the homework would be done! Alison had given up her evening class and her weekly swim at the Y, and she slept almost all of the weekend that her ex had the boys.*

*A psycho-educational assessment suggested that Simon had no specific learning problems, and he did not meet the criteria for a child with an attention deficit disorder. In fact, he was quite a bright young man whose academics were at least at grade level or beyond. His drawing of his family included his dad along with his mom and Sam, although he drew himself first and as the largest figure, firmly planted between the smaller parent figures but very close to Dad and with his back to Mom, with a tiny Sam hiding way off in a corner.*

*Alison and I pretty soon figured out that she was not in charge in the family. Simon was exhibiting quite a few controlling behaviours—not unusual in a child who is placed suddenly in the male "head of the household" role previously occupied by a now-absent dad. Rather than being aggressive and acting out, Simon was basically "on strike." He was using crying as a very powerful weapon that was being quite successful in backing off major authority figures, and he was able to keep his mom by his side for the majority of the evening by doing absolutely none of his required homework when she dared to walk away. He was also succeeding in keeping her away from Sam. Everyone was so concerned that he might "fail" at school that he was able to use the threat of failing as another powerful means of control.*

*This problem had to be approached in several different and careful ways. First of all, and most importantly, Alison decided that she **did** in fact want to take charge of her family again, despite the fact that she had little energy to do so. So we explored her goals for her children and herself, and managed to set up a small, basic set of expectations for family life that included some time for herself after the boys were in bed. We talked about what was and was not negotiable, and what choices and consequences there were in various situations. Simon and I spent time working with his feelings over the divorce and the fact that he missed his dad terribly. Alison became very adept at recognizing the controlling behaviours aimed at taking over her life and job as parent, and was able at some level to get the message across to Simon that she was indeed quite capable of being in charge of the major family decisions, including how to parent Sam, and that Simon was, in effect, "off duty" in that regard. She was also able to find a number of areas over which Simon **could** exercise control: choosing what he wears every day (even if it doesn't match),* *keeping his room the way he wants it (even if it's messy), learning to use the washing machine (even if he isn't very good at it), helping with groceries so he can learn to make his own lunches, and so on. Alison was now able to limit the time he spent on homework to the half hour his teacher agreed should suffice, using a timer instead of herself to indicate when his time is up, and fortunately his teacher agreed to take Simon to task when the homework was not done. His teacher also agreed to give Simon a very clear job description for when he was in the classroom, and to play a role in rewarding work that was completed independently. A self-monitoring program was put in place so that Simon could determine whether he was living up to his own goals each day, and he shared that with me when we met.*

*The overall situation has improved somewhat, although quite slowly. Alison still finds it very hard to be assertive in the face of bullying behaviour from males, even if they are much smaller than she is in size. She needs a lot of encouragement to stick to her guns and is receiving some therapeutic support to develop ways of dealing with situations in which she needs to remain the adult. Sam has his mom back. Simon seems to be happier; at least he is getting on with his work at school and his marks are improving, although he still has a long way to go as far as his father is concerned. He still wrestles his mom for control and tries to be the "man of the house" at the ripe old age of 10, basically going along with the unhealthy model that his dad provided for him. However, he is more willing to let go of the ball as long as Mom does not crumble and will run with it. Alison feels that she is back in the director's chair, even if it is hard work.*

## Permission to Parent

In the beginning, the message that emerged slowly and cautiously was one whereby parents appeared to be asking for permission to parent—permission to have rules and uphold them, permission to make use of their wider experiences to guide and teach their children, and most of all permission to govern the family without feeling that others were accusing them of fascism or abuse.

After a while, an analogy presented itself that seemed to fit the picture.

Running a family is akin to running a small business; there has to be a clear organizational structure, policies that govern the broad vision and mission of the company, procedures to make sure that the policies are carried out, and some system of management that leads to harmony within and a successful product as an outcome.

Thus arose the Family Management Model.

# 2

# The Family Management Model

We are going to look at one particular model of running a family—the *FAMILY MANAGEMENT MODEL*. This approach looks at managing families rather like running a small business, with management and trainees, and where the trainees are in fact training to become management, since one day, it is fervently hoped, they will leave the original company and go off to form a company of their own. We shall look at a number of different company structures, from the traditional two-manager company to the multi-merged company, find out about policies and procedures, job descriptions and negotiations—and examine different management styles that contribute to making parenting a unique job for each of us.

The Family Management Model is useful for family counselling and therapy, since it provides a framework within which any one of a number of different theoretical and clinical approaches can be incorporated. It can bridge the gap between therapeutic jargon and everyday experience for the vast majority of clients. Most importantly, it is a common-sense approach that can be used by individual families who would like to organize their own resources to put their own house in order.

The advantage of this model is that it enables each of us to determine what kind of family we want to run, what our own specific values are, what expectations we have, what parenting style we prefer, and what strategies we use. It can be used to identify and clarify the various roles of family members, to help to pinpoint where the system is running into problems, and to assist management in developing communication strategies for handling various types of problem situations. It provides a neutral language that is devoid of blame or fault, and encourages perceptions of difference, as opposed to right and wrong.

## Basic Assumptions

The approach to family management outlined in this book has its roots in a number of *basic assumptions*.

The first and most important of these assumptions is that, in families, *democracy does NOT work*. Parents have an obligation to make major decisions without the need for an electoral mandate. If children grow up believing that they have a right to an equal say in all decisions, they frequently develop an exaggerated sense of power and control.

Secondly, it is assumed that *children are not happy campers when they can boss parents around*. Children need to know their limits so that they can rebel happily and normally when they should be doing so. They need to be able to live with the security that parents know what they are doing (or can pretend they do!) and that they are protected by boundaries that do not move each and every time they are pushed or tested.

Thirdly, it is assumed that *family members are not created equal*. Parents have more power than children and must be prepared to make decisions. Those of us who have had more than one child know that each child is different from the others almost from the moment of conception. Therefore, it is not surprising that, in the family, children are not equal to each other — seniority and competence are alive and well, and individual differences are important. In fact, to treat all family members equally is not fair.

Finally, it is assumed that *parenting is not a gender issue*. Each individual is capable of nurturing, disciplining, decision making and general family management, regardless of genetic make-up or traditional roles. Thus, throughout this entire book, it is rare to find a distinction drawn between mothers and fathers, males and females.

## Total Quality Management

In the successfully managed family, Total Quality Management (TQM) is practised — *all members of the company are nurtured and empowered in areas where they have expertise, and are coached and trained in areas where they do not.* Whenever a new skill is learned under supervision, the individual is permitted to try it out alone, provided circumstances are safe and legal. Once mastery is established, responsibility and accountability follow.

No one is fired and no one quits. These options are sometimes threatened in companies where the structure is temporarily weakened (and remains weakened until they are off the company agenda). The family company does not function well under either form of blackmail.

No one is paid money for being a member of the family; reinforcement takes other forms. There is a long-term commitment to and bond among all members of the company. When such a bond is broken (for example, if the managers decide to form separate companies) there is a major change in the perception of loyalties within the company.

Although most managers face class-action suits and strikes from time to time, there are no unions and no formal collective bargaining within the family company. This is because all family members are treated as individuals, with unequal wants and needs, and therefore the disadvantages of lumping the children together as one unit far outweigh the advantages. There are frequently situations where separate procedures are required for management and for trainees, and not all trainees need the same procedures to fulfill their roles within the family company.

## Goals of Family Management

Apart from the general aim of providing a pleasant, nurturing environment in which individual company members can develop to their fullest potential, the goal of the family company is to coach and educate trainees to the point where they can leave to become managers in a company of their own. In other words, the family is really a *management training company*. This can be an extremely useful goal to keep in mind particularly when parenting older teens, since most parents are reluctant to give up responsibility for continuing to shape and influence their product, and yet they realize that the old ways of parenting younger children are no longer effective and frequently result in conflict. There is thus a need to change management strategies as the trainees develop competencies of their own, shifting from orders to advice as the focus of accountability changes with time.

The main responsibilities of management in this company are as follows:

1. To maintain the family as a viable entity by making a long-term commitment to the well-being of all members;
2. To be the "architects" of the family by taking responsibility for the overall plan and by setting policies and procedures in line with that plan;
3. To bring up the children in a nurturing, safe environment that is supportive during their training as emerging but very inexperienced adults;
4. To help to teach children to become fully functioning adults who have a set of independent living skills so that they may leave the family company and know how to keep themselves healthy and safe;
5. To be willing to evaluate the job that they are doing on a regular basis, and to refine and change it where necessary, to accommodate individual needs, developmental changes and diverse crises.

Seems like a big job, doesn't it? It's almost like breathing—when you think about it too much, you can't do it, so you try to forget and just get on with things.

It is not normally necessary to talk to parents about the need to love children; we all KNOW that. In fact, loving a child is one of the most intense emotions we will ever be privileged to feel and for the most part is not too difficult to achieve. However, the intensity of emotion in *any* relationship usually has both a positive AND a negative side—and those we love the most we frequently hate the most. There are times for parents when we not only question whether we LIKE a particular child, we may actually question our commitment to, or love for, that same child. This is a devastating place to be, but one that is sometimes frighteningly familiar. A standard, first-response line is to dislike the "behaviour" not the child, and this can certainly get us out of this corner on occasion. However, in my business and in my personal life, I frequently encounter people who REALLY DO NOT LIKE one or more of their children, and who would much rather opt out of the job of parenting, thank you very much. It's hard to MAKE people love their children, since we learn the hard way that we cannot control other people's feelings. Suffice it to say that loving and liking your trainees will certainly make the job of family management easier. But, whether or not you love or like them, there is still a job to be done in terms of parenting them. Hopefully, this model enables all of us to get on with that job, however we feel about it. Generally, when things run smoothly, when management is back in charge, and when trainees are content with their job descriptions and the approval cooperation brings, the ground is fertile for liking and loving to begin to grow again.

The remainder of this book deals with various aspects of family management—from the basic structure of the family that affects everyone's roles, to management styles, through policies and procedures, to various management strategies and issues of labour relations. Here we go...

# 3

# The Structure of the Family Company

## Democracy or Dictatorship?

In families, as in small businesses, where many difficult decisions need to be made for the long-term viability of the individuals and the system, democracy is highly inefficient, breeds conflict and does not work. At least, it seems to work only under certain circumstances:

1. when there are two parents with solidarity and an only child who can always be outvoted; this may result, however, in a child who feels completely powerless;
2. when you have two parents and two children, one of whom always votes against the other, regardless of the issue; this, however, perpetuates and exacerbates sibling conflict;
3. when you are pretty certain that everyone will agree (as in "Who wants to leave the chores and go have fun?"); in fact, this may well be the only situation in which a democratic approach can be used successfully.

Democracy rarely works in single parent families (especially in the one child/one parent combination) or in families where there are significant marital conflicts, and never in families where the children outnumber the parents.

27

**Rather, the approach that seems to work best is a hierarchical one where the PARENTS take a definite leadership role as the directors of the company, and the philosophy more closely approximates that of a Benign Dictatorship.**

This approach does not mean that children's feelings or opinions are never considered important—of course they are. Changes may well be made within the family based on suggestions or opinions from the children, but the changes are made advisedly following due consideration, not simply as a short-term reaction to a current temporary unhappiness. There are many family decisions that would never be made if we waited for our children's blessing—the TV would never go off, vegetable farmers would go out of business, homework would never be done, and life would be a continuous holiday.

It never ceases to amaze me how guilty parents feel about establishing themselves at the head of the family company. Somewhere along the way, they seem to have received the message that children should always be part of the decision making, and that the only acceptable decisions are those that keep children happy. In the long run, our children will be happiest when they have parents who are willing to carry out the parenting role.

Given that democracy is seldom workable, how then DO we get families to function well? The following family had worked for many years under a one-person-one-vote approach to family problem solving.

 *A family I met many moons ago had arrived at a complete impasse. The 16-year-old son had decided to drop out of school, and his 14-year-old sister was firmly on his side—partly to keep her own options open for later, and partly because her support kept him in Mom and Dad's bad books. The vote on whether he should or should not be permitted to leave school was a 2-2 split. Because they had always worked on the one-person-one-vote philosophy, the family had no way of resolving the dilemma and had sought some mediation. With some effort on my part to hide the incredulity that they seemed to have managed for 16 years or more with a purely democratic approach, we began to explore their history of problem solving within the family. It turned out that, some three years previously, there had been another major family vote when Mom had decided that she wanted to return to*

*the work force. She had been outvoted 3-1, and had remained at home, becoming increasingly angry and resentful. Once we had worked at abandoning the democratic approach, and dealt with establishing a hierarchy within the family, we were able to reinstate the rights of management to make decisions in some key, non-negotiable areas, and the family was able to approach the problem from a different perspective. The original vote was nullified, the son remained in school—and Mom went out to work.*

**The Family Management Model involves a DEFINITE and PERMANENT HIERARCHY that will never change within any given family.**

## Management and Trainees

Family members are not created equal, and parents must be prepared to assume the decision-making role because of their experience. Parents therefore form the "**management**" of the company, and children are the valued "**trainees**."

The purpose of the family company is to educate, coach and encourage the trainees to be skilled enough eventually to go out and form a company of their own. Thus, in functional families, the trainees NEVER become managers in their original company, even when they are quite capable of management, unless or until such time as their original managers become senile and/or incapacitated.

Families are no different from any other small group. Leaders will emerge in a natural fashion. This means that if parents are unable or unwilling to perform the leadership role, a child will take over. There is no minimum age at which this occurs. There are some moms or dads or couples who become slaves to a newborn from the minute he comes home from the hospital. I have met many families where a child as young as two has been in charge. Parents may be heard to complain: "We can't go out because she won't stay with a babysitter" or "We have no time to ourselves because he insists on staying up until we go to bed." There are single parents who "cannot" date, and older siblings who "have to" have the same bedtime or allowance as a bossy younger child. Sound familiar?

Believe it or not, children are not happy being management. It is quite frightening when people that we assumed knew what they were doing and were in charge in fact turn out not to be, and when we have to take over a situation when we don't have sufficient knowledge or experience, or don't see or understand the "big picture." Many parents will recognize that the child who wrestles the power is frequently angry or depressed or both—in any event, not a happy camper.

*Pat and Martin had waited many long years to have their only child, a daughter named Jessica. Both highly educated professionals, they had delayed pregnancy and then had more difficulty than they had expected conceiving. Jess was thus a belated but much loved trainee for these highly competent individuals. They had gone to great lengths to provide her with everything she wanted, and she had grown up with the message that her every wish was their command. Jess was having major tantrums at home, to the point where both parents were intimidated and dreading confrontations with her. At school, she was quite unpopular with the other children. She desperately wanted to be included in social activities with her peers, but (as is the case with many girls in the mid-elementary grades) the cliques were formed and she was firmly excluded. When we met, she was 11 years old, and the family was in turmoil.*

*Our first meeting included both parents and Jess. It soon become obvious who was in control in this family. Every time Mom opened her mouth, Jess either interrupted extraordinarily rudely, or else sat with her arms folded, giving Mom "The Look." Dad said nothing until invited to do so, at which point he whispered "I don't know why I'm here," and huddled back into his corner of the sofa. As I traditionally do, I asked the family who was in charge— who was management. While both Mom and Dad managed to stutter around to the fact that they perhaps should be, all three conceded in their own way that in reality Jess was. When asked if this was how they wanted it, of course two of them said no, while the other glared at all of us in turn and chose not to respond.*

*We discussed the assumptions of the Family Management Model under which we would work if we were to work together. Both parents agreed that Jess was definitely not happy and was frequently out of control at home and now also at school— a big factor in her relationships with her teachers and her peers who, of course, would not take on the servant role she not only expected, but demanded. They agreed that their family was NOT a democracy; in fact, Jess made the majority of the decisions! They would have been much happier even with one-person-one-vote, since that would have ensured management control, and yet they were both quite apprehensive, to say the least, about their ability to shift to this position in the face of the vehement opposition they both anticipated. Mom and Dad had a rather uneven division of labour when it came to parenting, with Mom taking almost the full share of the role (as Dad put it, "She's human resources, I'm physical plant") but neither was interested in changing that aspect of management. They did, however, show a great deal of interest in trying to reestablish a management hierarchy at home with some support at our "management only" sessions. It was a very important message to Jess that she was NOT invited to these sessions—a rule she did not like and actively, albeit vainly, fought. It was also a message to her parents that I would not be the one to take over the parenting by telling Jess what she should be doing. However, she had her own day in court later on in some individual sessions, and we met once or twice as a group, simply to monitor progress and to troubleshoot.*

*Over the course of six months, Jess and her parents learned to identify and openly to label her "Queen of Hearts" behaviour: her demanding tone, her "off-with-his-head!" attitude when things don't go her way, her attempts to be management, her inappropriate ordering around of Mom and Dad in front of others, and her temper tantrums. She has had a hard time recognizing her body language—the folded arms, the stuck-out chin, "The Look"—but this is coming along. Mom has calmly reestablished the hierarchy and has been learning to support Dad when he mildly does the same (on occasion!). They have become comfortable giving Jess a set of choices and no longer allow their guilt to get in the way of allowing her to follow through with what she chooses, even when the consequences of her choices are unpleasant for her. While there are still many power struggles at home, things at school have settled. Jess now has a teacher who is far more confident than the previous one was in being "management" in the classroom, and so Jess's tactics do not work and her classmates have observed a different attitude. She has been invited to several birthday parties over the past couple of months and was able to invite ten girls to her own. We are now able to concentrate on self-esteem issues, such as body image and social skills, that are important for Jess.*

**Managers never need to apologize for managing.**

**It is a basic assumption of the Family Management approach that a happy child is one whose limits are understandable, predictable and reasonably consistently applied, and whose responsibilities are clearly age-appropriate and within the boundaries of his ability level.**

# Variations In Management Structure

Various management structures exist depending on: the number of managers (one, two, more than two); whether management is full-time or part-time; whether trainees are full-time or part-time; whether trainees are there by virtue of birth, or are chosen or imposed; and whether there are multi-generations of managers involved. This may result in a great deal of confusion on the part of trainees in particular as to who precisely is in charge of what and where.

## Traditional Structure

The traditional family structure still prevails, despite media efforts to make us believe differently. This is one in which there are two original managers who founded the company, and one or more trainees. The managers have made a commitment to each other to stay together for life, which makes it much easier to ride out the fluctuations in harmony that naturally occur over the course of many decades, since individual management decisions can be made in the context of the issue at hand and are not seen as decisions as to whether or not the company is viable, or whether or not one manager will stay or leave. In addition, trainees are never put in the traumatic position of feeling responsible for a company dissolution, nor are they ever required to take the responsibility for the continued viability of the management team. Such a company structure provides stability and security for its trainees, along with a wide range of models of problem-solving strategies and styles.

## Single Manager Companies

As we all know, there are many situations in which there is only one manager in a family company. This may occur for one of three reasons.

**(a) Conscious choice:** This can take one of a number of forms. The first is the situation in which an individual (overwhelmingly a female) decides to produce and manage trainees with only a small deposit from a disinterested party to help set off the process. Another is where a manager from a traditional company decides that the stresses of managing alone are far preferable to the conflicts of attempting to manage together, so takes the trainees and leaves. Yet another is where both managers decide they have had enough and agree to form two separate companies, each (initially at least) with a single manager.

In all of these forms, the decision to manage alone was made voluntarily by the individual who accepts the management responsibilities, at least in theory and at least initially. The attitudes of managers in these situations is usually quite positive, active and sometimes even defiantly defensive of the decision.

**(b) By default:** This can take one of several forms. The first is the situation where one of the managers decides he or she has had enough of the job and goes off to sample the delights of an aerobics instructor called Tiffany or a sensitive lawyer called Chad. Another is the individual who decides that the need to "find oneself" far outweighs the burdens of marriage and children. In these situations, the remaining manager not only feels abandoned, but is frequently required to give up, against his or her will, full-time parenting to relinquish the children part-time to a departing partner who has never shown much interest in the human resources aspects of the company. Another scenario is the partner who is left behind by the parent who has unilaterally decided to take the kids and leave, and who decides to fight for the right to continue to manage the original trainees. In none of these situations is the remaining partner a willing or happy camper. In the cases where the partner who has left shows little or no interest in continuing to share the management responsibilities, there is usually deep indignation at being left with the whole load. It takes a great deal of determination to remain in charge of the trainees in the face of such inner resentment.

**(c) By higher power:** A far different alternative to all the others is the situation in which one of the managing partners dies and the other is left to manage alone with much sadness and an empty chair at the board room table. The remaining partner may sometimes abdicate the management position in order to deal with what are seen as far more pressing emotional and practical survival issues—and children are frequently required to put aside their own emotional needs to take on more responsibility for helping to run the family than their developmental level would normally accommodate. While the overwhelming feelings may be of loneliness and sadness, there is also frequently some anger and resentment at being abandoned. It is sometimes quite difficult for any replacement manager who may be brought in at a later date to manage in his or her own way because of the shadow of the previous individual whose role and attributes may have become somewhat idealized.

Trainees in a single-manager company tend to assume positions of greater importance than in traditional structures, and frequently outnumber the manager. They are much more likely, therefore, to take on management-type roles, including caretaking, advice giving, policy setting, personnel management, finance critic, and so on, and may find it extremely difficult to relinquish such roles if or when there is another change in family structure. Single managers are more likely to struggle with management hierarchy issues simply because they do not have committed back-up. However, as in traditional family structures, parents have to decide to be managers and be convinced that this is what the children need before the message even begins to filter through to the trainees, let alone begins to be believed.

## Branch Offices and Restructured Companies

Once a single manager merges with a manager from another company, all manner of structures are possible. There may be two individual parents from previously formed families, each with children of his or her own; these children may be part-time in two different companies, or full-time in one. There may be one partner who has existing children while the other one has none. Both parents from the original company may merge with other partners, and then both may have part-time trainees from two different companies at different times. It gets even more complicated when the newly formed partnership produces a full-time trainee of its own, displacing everyone else in status in this particular company. Some children whose original parents have both merged and produced offspring in new families are "floaters" who sometimes feel that they do not belong in either of the new companies. Even at best, loyalties are divided.

## Replacement Managers

Whatever the reason for the departure of one of the original partners, the role of a replacement manager is a complex and difficult one. This individual may need to take back some of the responsibilities that were thrust on or taken over by one or more of the trainees who may have come to assume ownership in these areas. For example, the most senior trainee may have assumed the role of confidante or adviser to the single manager, may have taken on some of the parenting responsibilities for younger siblings, or generally may have become a junior manager in a number of subtle ways. Thus, children frequently react to any perceived move on the part of their own parent or the individual whom they see as a potential replacement management partner to reduce their level of power and control by changing roles within the family structure. In families, new brooms do not sweep clean—they stir up all the hidden dust bunnies.

Replacement parents cannot be expected to be committed to someone else's children in the same way they are to their own. Therefore, it is at least as important, if not more so, in a restructured company for the management team to work hard on policies and procedures, which will be dealt with in subsequent chapters. This is so that the trainees, be they part-time or full-time, know the general philosophies of the company and what their own particular jobs are, separate from the feelings and loyalties that may or may not exist or develop within the restructured company.

## "Interfere-iority"

The effects of such complex variations in management structure on children and the stress that results cannot be overemphasized. Their stability and security are threatened, and their job descriptions are often unclear, differing depending upon location. One of the most significant sources of stress is when the manager of one of their two companies is trying to tell the manager of the other company how that company should be run (in the interests of the trainees, of course) This is made even worse when the trainees are responsible in any way, shape or form for transmitting this helpful advice and reporting on the reactions to it.

In the overwhelming number of cases of branch companies, as we have seen, at least one of the original partners is not pleased. This is a phenomenal understatement in many situations. There seems to be a compelling need for some partners to continue to attempt to run the company they have decided to leave, or to dictate to the manager who has quit how he or she should be running his or her new company.

As long as trainees are not being abused or neglected (and the Children's Aid Society is the only agency with the mandate to determine whether this is indeed the case) there does not seem to be a "right" and a "wrong" way to run a company. It is just **DIFFERENT**. Managers from other companies may well see a more efficient way of doing things; however, this still does not mean that it is right. "Interfere-iority" in the running of a new company by a manager from the original company can perpetuate the unhappiness of trainees who are probably quite capable of learning that they have slightly different jobs in the two companies. As with most employees, children work best in a situation where each of the managers has provided them with a clear job description and an outline of the policies of the company, and where the managers are willing to support and encourage trainee/management relations.

## Part-time Trainees

Even with the best of intentions on the part of management, part-time trainees do have a particularly difficult time. They have to learn to live with several different sets of policies from the various managers involved, along with procedures that may differ depending upon the person upholding them. Providing their job descriptions are clear, and provided the individual managers act consistently *within* themselves, children may adapt to some degree of variability between locations and managers. In an effort to regain some of the control they have lost when the original family broke up, many part-time trainees may try to take over one or other company. Sometimes, because we, as parents, feel very sorry for part-time trainees, we let them. They have neither the skills nor the experience, so they are highly likely to fail, and then we wonder why they lose their sense of self-worth.

One major problem for children who participate on a part-time basis in more than one family is that they are sometimes used as couriers from one manager to another. Even separated parents who swear that they do not communicate with each other through the children frequently do not recognize that messages are indeed carried back and forth, verbal or non-verbal, and that children may often be struggling as much with NOT talking about what happens in the other company as with what they should say. The original company still has business to be conducted and this will continue until each of the children becomes independent enough to start a company of his or her own.

**It is vitally important for the mental health of the children that separated parents develop a means of communicating with each other that completely eliminates the involvement of the children, even if it means having management meetings off company property.**

## Parent Companies—or "Management Consultants"

One continuing blip in the smooth running of family companies can occur when there are visits from managers of your own parent company or, worse, from managers of your partner's parent company. This may place each of us in the difficult position of feeling like a trainee again, at the same time as management decisions need to be made in our own company. Our parents, of course, played a big role in training us, and do not always understand why we have modified, jettisoned or otherwise adapted some of their training techniques. They are frequently not afraid to comment (again, verbally or non-verbally) on how we are carrying out our duties, or to offer suggestions as to how we might work more efficiently. There are few among us who are brave enough to thank our former managers for their excellent training and guidance, and to inform them we are now quite confident and competent in the running of our own company.

**It is useful to think of our former managers as "consultants," since they will never be in charge of running our company, any more than we will ever be in charge of running theirs.**

It is comforting to have experienced managers "on call," so to speak, especially when we encounter the new situations or endless crises that seem to be part of a management training company. Calling in the "consultants" can be extremely useful, as most managing directors know, and they can frequently offer insights from a slight distance that can add to our perspective on a particular issue. It helps if we are open to acknowledging their points of view, whether or not we feel we can incorporate them into our solution to the problem. However, when our consultants have an emotional investment in how we function, since it reflects directly on whether or not they did their original job well, their advice may frequently be biased. They may be overly critical or overly forgiving—or may prefer to blame the other half of our management team, since they can distance themselves very nicely from any responsibility for that individual's management approach.

As we raise our children, we may face for the first time the depth of differences between how we were ourselves raised and how our partner was raised. This may lead to an increased understanding of these differences along with greater tolerance for them, or it may lead to increased conflict if we each choose to defend our parent company's approach.

In situations where former managers are living on our company premises, it is important to be careful that everyone recognizes who the bosses are in our company, and to acknowledge that grandparents have a very important, but different, role to play in the lives of our trainees. This distinction becomes very difficult when we as parents have never in fact emotionally "left" the original family company to become committed to our own.

 *Tony was a nine-year-old boy referred to my office by his school principal for being openly defiant to his teachers and refusing to do his work in the classroom or any homework that was sent home. He lived with his mom and his maternal grandparents. Grandma stayed home all day and spoke only Italian, despite having lived in an English-speaking community for a number of years, while Grandpa was bilingual and worked long hours as a construction worker.*

*Mom had left an abusive relationship with Dad when Tony was only a year or so old, and had been living with her parents and a huge dose of Catholic guilt ever since. She lived in fear that Dad, who had not been heard from in a number of years, would come back and kidnap Tony and/or assault her. She worked shifts as a cleaner in a hotel—a steady, stable job but very poorly paid. Grandma ran the home with an iron fist without the velvet glove, except she pandered to her grandson's every need. Tony never had*

*to raise a finger to do anything; Grandma would tidy his toys, pick up his clothes, cook something different for him if he didn't like what was served for dinner, change the TV channel on demand, and so on. (We all know how his last servant died.) While Grandma would complain endlessly about Tony's behaviour, any disciplining was left to Mom.*

*The problem was that Tony's mom was completely powerless in this family structure. Whatever attempts she made to take charge of her son, or even to take care of him, were undermined completely by Grandma who alternately criticized her daughter openly, countermanded her daughter's decisions or took over tasks that Tony had been given to do and completed them for him.*

*When I met them, Tony had reached a stage where he was at best ignoring Mom and at worst being emotionally, verbally and occasionally physically abusive. He presented himself as a very sullen and angry young man with low self-esteem who seemed to be quite anxious about the likelihood of having to repeat his grade in school. Mom was worried about the constant calls from school and was at a loss as to know what to do to change the school situation. It became clear early in the first session with Mom and Tony that they both saw Grandma as being in charge of the family company at home, and that Mom did not see herself as "management" at all. Whatever he may have said about her being in charge, Tony's view of Grandma's job was, however, that she was there to meet his needs, and he clearly saw Mom as someone who interfered with this constantly! Grandma in no way backed up Mom's attempts at management; in fact, Mom recognized that she felt quite incompetent in matters of the family when her mother was around. Grandpa was completely out of the picture, except for providing Tony with a male role model who also appeared to have his every need indulged.*

*This was a difficult situation to deal with because, even apart from the language barriers, Grandma had no interest whatsoever in becoming involved in family counselling since she felt that this was a problem with the school and nothing more. It was obvious that nothing at home would change until the time came when Mom could decide to take over management of her own small, two-person company and would have the confidence to determine her own policies and procedures for Tony. Until such a change was made, Tony would continue to have no respect for authority, especially when the authority figure was a female, and would not see himself as having tasks to complete independently.*

*While Mom seemed almost ready to tackle this situation, she simply could not commit to taking time off without pay for therapy sessions. Perhaps most importantly, however, she had become quite resigned to being abused to some degree or other by most people in her family environment, including her nine-year-old son, and was feeling very overwhelmed by the enormity of the task ahead.*

*It was pretty obvious that we could all hold our collective breaths until we turned blue if we waited for a system change in this family. Therefore, the school situation was dealt with on a straightforward behavioural basis in rather a superficial fashion, using a positive job description for Tony with suitable incentives for compliance. The following year, he was transferred to a class with a male teacher, and Mom's anxiety was alleviated to some extent. What, unfortunately, did not change was Tony's attitude to women or Mom's sense of power as a person and as a parent.*

## The Importance of Stability

There is little question that instability in family structure causes tremendous confusion and anxiety among trainees. However "dysfunctional" an existing company might be seen to be by one or both managers, and however much managers might justify change as being in the best interests of the children, any alteration in structure is highly stressful at the time it occurs, and ramifications may continue over a period of years. Children from families whose structure has changed in some major way almost universally wish for a return to the original setup—even many years later, even if the change occurred early on in their lifetime and, interestingly, even if they appear to be quite content with the new management/trainee structure. They generally continue to crave contact with both original managers, however "absent" one of the managers may be, and do not seem to discriminate between "good" and "bad" management approaches, until such time as they need to protect themselves from chronic disappointment. Managers give up on trainees long before trainees give up on management.

However, management decisions must be made—and trainees can and do cope.

**4**

# Management Style

## Right, Wrong—or Simply Different?

Of all the issues involved in managing the family company, management style is arguably the one that causes the most conflict and absorbs the most energy from parents. The major problem is that generally we did not choose our management partner based on his or her parenting style—we chose them based on personality, looks, character, whatever—and frequently we chose them because they are DIFFERENT from ourselves.

During the first phase of a relationship, before we even contemplate starting a company or taking on trainees, we usually have some inkling that differences can be both intriguing and irritating. We then proceed to spend inordinate amounts of time and effort trying to change the other person by endeavouring to get them to understand that doing things *our* way is in fact not only beneficial, but also infinitely sensible.

We also tend to confuse "different" with "wrong" or "inferior." For example, at the very beginning of my partnership, I was astounded to find out from my helpful other half that there was a right and a wrong way to cut grapefruit and top an egg. To this day I do not know how anyone could have existed for 25 years without knowing that! For my part, I also discovered early on that there were ways of squeezing the toothpaste out of the tube other than starting in the middle, ridiculous and wrong though those ways may be. It takes a long time and a deep commitment to work through the differences and to blend and meld them to form a composite whole.

Imagine, if your company can flounder on toothpaste and eggs, what havoc is wrought by the introduction of trainees and the need to find a common approach to management. No wonder children are the focus of so much conflict in relationships.

So let's get one thing straight very early here. We are NOT going to waste any time waiting around until you and your management partner agree on management style. You are two different people. You will always be two different people. You got together because you are two different people. Your children know you are two different people. Having children does not change your personality too noticeably (other than to bring out even more negative stuff, like rage, intolerance and impatience). So we shall all be six feet under ground before we can be identical in our management style.

So what about the notion of consistency that we've all heard about from all kinds of sources? Don't parents need to be consistent? Yes, of course, in terms of policies and procedures, and in what we expect of our children. This is so they don't go completely crazy trying to dance to a number of different drummers. But HOW we go about maintaining this consistency is up for grabs.

Children are amazingly tolerant of a number of things, not the least of which is the fact that both their parents have different ways of going about things. I have been able to ascertain from three-year-olds which parent they would go to for the soft touch, and which one is the most predictable. Teenagers are experts at this. Understanding parental styles and being able to predict them is something that gives children a real sense of control, sometimes in the good sense of control that serves to reduce their anxiety, and sometimes in the sense of power that doesn't always feel quite right. Nonetheless, given that they are aware at a very young age of your differences and that they can use that understanding to help them predict and control their world, the need for consistency between your styles takes on less importance. In fact, it provides your trainees with an opportunity to experience two different leadership styles and to develop a range of coping strategies.

 *Jennifer was a young, very attractive woman who came in to discuss her son Jason, aged seven. He was being threatened with expulsion from Grade 2 because of some aggressive behaviour, including biting other children. Further exploration revealed that life at home was not exactly peaceful. Jennifer had been married*

*to Tim since shortly after high school, and they had moved very quickly into having a family—a lot more quickly, in fact, than either of them had planned. There were now three boys in their family, ranging in age from five to nine, and all of them were acting out to some degree. Jason was at the point of beating up on Mom as well as his brothers whenever Dad was out of the house, and she had the bruises to prove it. When Dad was home, there was little or no aggression, apparently, on the part of any of the boys. As usual in situations such as this, Mom was both resentful and envious of Dad's ability to keep control, and was heavily into guilt about her feelings of wanting to leave all of them to it and go off somewhere. Also it became apparent that there were some marital difficulties that had nothing to do with the children, but were clearly affecting Jennifer's ability to trust Tim and contributing to her feelings of wanting to pack it all in and start over. Her energy level was extremely low, to the point where we discussed the possibility of a depression, and she looked to all intents and purposes like a deflated balloon. We tried to discuss the need to have an immediate Zero Tolerance of Violence rule in effect and enforced both at home and at school so that the seriousness of Jason's situation would become obvious to him. It became obvious very quickly that there seemed to be many issues getting in the way of implementing this pretty straightforward piece of legislation, the primary one being that Jennifer did not see herself as having nearly enough control or strength to outrank her seven-year-old son.*

*Tim came in with Jennifer for the next session so that we could discuss the management of this family company, since I had made it clear that I could not start to work with one of the trainees until it became clear to me what the family company was all about. What were the structures?, who was in charge of what?, what were the main policies?, and what did they want Jason's job description to be, other than resident Pit Bull? In contrast to Jennifer's deflated balloon, or what Barbara Coloroso would call "jellyfish," Tim was the "brick wall." He was remarkably sure of what he was doing with the boys, and treated Jennifer's concerns with something a little shy of contempt. He clearly saw her as ineffective, and wasted little time telling me so—not quite in so many words, but the message was clear to all of us. If ONLY she would do things HIS way (i.e., the RIGHT way) everything would be fine. According to him, you just had to say "do it!" and it was done. None of this persuading and bribing stuff—just a raised voice and a swift swat on the butt, and there was no trouble from any of the boys. He saw Jennifer as endlessly nagging, pursuing, yelling, cajoling, and eventually giving in just to keep the peace. Jennifer, on the other hand, found the energy to point out that he came down on the boys like a ton of bricks, and was never interested in listening to what they had to say or how they felt or why they had done what they had done. She espoused the view that you catch more flies with honey than with vinegar; unfortunately, the jar had been empty for a very long time. They spent almost the whole session arguing about who was doing things how, and they were each quite determined that their way was right and that the other's way was wrong, finally coming to the conclusion that they couldn't agree on anything.*

*When we started to work through Jason's current situation from the Family Management viewpoint, several issues became clearer. The structure of the family was quite secure, despite some marital difficulties, and they both had a clear and solid commitment to each other and to the boys. When we talked policy regarding Jason's behaviour, they were both absolutely in favour of zero tolerance for violence because aggression was not, in their value system, an appropriate way of getting what you want. While they felt this strongly, it became evident that they had not explained this policy very well to the boys, since the boys' view was that you didn't use violence because you'd get into trouble if you did. Certainly younger children will modify their behaviour depending upon the consequences, rather than the deeper reason, but it helps them to know the big picture, in brief summary form at least. They also had exactly the same procedures in place in terms of using a reasonably consistent time-out routine that worked well for Jason if they could get him to his room. What was different was how they went about enforcing the procedures in terms of their management style. Jennifer would try to persuade Jason to agree that going to time-out was a better idea than beating up his brother, and unfortunately he would not agree with this. So she would continue to try to change his mind until the storm broke. Which it inevitably did. Even when she managed to get him into time-out, she would then be back and forth to his room, trying to persuade him that it was not a good idea to be upset, that she had been fully justified in putting him there, and frequently she apologized for having to do so. On the other hand, Tim did not waste any time. As soon as Jason's behaviour started to deteriorate, he immediately initiated the time-out process, by physically taking him to his room if he had to. As Jennifer had described, he spent no time at all on feelings or motivations or any other discussion. Although this approach worked at the time to discourage such behaviours when Tim was around, it did not appear to be teaching Jason that in general the aggressive behaviour was not acceptable at ANY time; he had simply learned not to get caught when Tim was there. From Jennifer he had learned that he could get away (almost) with murder.*

*Once we had established that there were, in fact, large areas in which the two of them actually agreed, including what they wanted changed about the current situation with Jason, it was easier to work together on the issues around behaviour and even to establish a positive connection with Jason's teacher, who also had similar goals. Up to that point, Jennifer had felt blamed and inadequate when she had had contact with the school. When we looked at the issues from the point of view of what Jason needed to know and what his job description was in given situations (for example, when he got really mad at his mom or his younger brother), they were able to establish a set of choices for Jason that would result in certain consequences that he himself would choose. In other words, if he chose to start a certain behaviour, he would be choosing to be put in his room for a few minutes. Looking at it this way enabled Jennifer to follow through more consistently, since she could persuade herself that in fact he had known that that was what would happen, and had been given the chance to make a different choice. This seemed to help her give herself permission to back off the endless verbalizing, and to act with some confidence. Tim was able to see that Jason needed some education about his behaviour along with the consequences, and was able to take advantage of some quiet times to discuss some general issues of how to solve problems in the form of reading books or telling stories or simply talking over day-to-day happenings. Jennifer and Tim began to support each other instead of competing, and things actually improved at home fairly quickly, with both parents much more able to support the teacher's efforts in the classroom. Last I heard, Jason had made it to Grade 3.*

When a child clearly understands that a particular behaviour is inappropriate and you have explained in simple terms why, there is no purpose whatever in taking time to reexplain it every time. If a child does not agree that the behaviour is inappropriate or does not appear to care about a consequence, there is little utility in waiting for a change of mind, especially if the behaviour is threatening in any way. However, we know from quite a body of research that when children are given a reason for a consequence, they tend to be more willing to comply with a rule or expectation, and the compliance tends to extend from one specific circumstance to a range of similar circumstances, whether or not an authority figure is present. In situations like Jennifer and Tom's, it is very difficult not to sound as if you are supporting one parent's style over the other. This is true especially in families where management appears to be in some form of competition with each other and any statement of support means "I won!" Some styles work better in some circumstances. Some styles work better on some days. Some styles work better with some children in some circumstances on some days. In other words, there's no RIGHT style.

## The Two Way Street of Parenting Styles

Many years ago, an American psychologist by the name of Diana Birnbaum and some of her colleagues conducted some seminal research looking at children's behaviour that resulted from particular parenting styles. They found that certain ways of parenting appeared to be related to fairly predictable behaviours in the children of those families. They also postulated that there were two main dimensions of parenting styles that interacted to form four distinct parenting styles. One dimension was concerned with parental *feelings* towards the child and ranged on a continuum that at one extreme represented emotional coldness, rejection and distance and at the other extreme represented emotional warmth, acceptance and closeness. The second dimension was more concerned with the extent to which the family was governed by **rules or expectations**, at the one extreme being highly restrictive and structured, and at the other being extremely permissive and unstructured. When these two dimensions were combined, they resulted in four distinct management styles:

*Dismissive:*       permissive/cold/rejecting
*Laissez-faire:*    permissive/warm/accepting

*Authoritarian:*     restrictive/cold/rejecting
*Authoritative:*     restrictive/warm/accepting.

When the different child behaviours were clustered under the different parenting styles, the results were as follows:

## DISMISSIVE
### Permissive/Cold/Rejecting
No rules or rules not upheld; distant, aloof manager

**General characteristics of trainees:**
no respect for authority; no sense of self-respect
*independent, often "street-smart"*
*rebellious*
*disobedient*
*aggressive, maybe violent*
*delinquent*
*no conscience*
*no remorse*
*lack of self-control*

## LAISSEZ-FAIRE
### Permissive/Warm/Accepting
No rules or rules not upheld; warm, fuzzy manager

**General characteristics of trainees:**
little respect for authority; awareness of "self"
*independent*
*outgoing*
*sense of self-worth*
*active*
*assertive*
*friendly, tolerant*
*expects equality with adults*
*can turn into a "spoiled brat"*

## AUTHORITARIAN
### Restrictive/Cold/Rejecting
Lots of rules; distant, aloof manager

**General characteristics of trainees:**
constrained by authority; no sense of self-respect or autonomy
*may comply when parent
    is around*
*socially withdrawn*
*sullen*
*quarrelsome*
*inhibited*
*inability to express feelings*
*withdrawn, depressed*
*lack of initiative*

## AUTHORITATIVE
### Restrictive/Warm/Accepting
Lots of rules; warm, fuzzy manager

**General characteristics of trainees:**
constrained by authority; awareness of "self"
*may comply even when parent
    is not around*
*generally well-adjusted*
*relies on structure*
*polite*
*obedient, compliant*
*dependent*
*submissive*
*"overprotected"*

There are several important issues that emerge from this apparently simple model.

Each of us, as a manager and as a parent, tends to have a "preferred" style. I know you have been thinking that you definitely fall somewhere between the "*Laissez-faire*" and the "Authoritative"—with the best components of both. In reality, although we may have a particular natural way of doing things, each individual's management style can change, not only from day to day, but also from trainee to trainee and from situation to situation. In other words, on one particular occasion with one particular child when you are in a certain mood or frame of mind, you may well be able to be Authoritative. At another time, you may have had a bad day at work, the children may have been getting on your nerves from the moment you walked in the door—and suddenly you become Authoritarian or Dismissive. As your style changes, so do the behaviours exhibited by the children. When you suddenly become Authoritarian, especially if you are generally *Laissez-faire*, your children will not only notice, but they will react. Sometimes quite dramatically. The bouncy, assertive, "I'm in charge!" trainee may suddenly become sullen, withdrawn and downright hostile. As you change styles again, the behaviour will change again.

The way we act as managers influences how our trainees respond, and the way our trainees act influences how *we* respond.

This suggests that the way our children are behaving will encourage us to use a particular parenting style, whether or not it is our natural preference, and this may constantly be changing. For example, if our children are having a good day, are being polite, compliant, and generally well-adjusted (don't you wish!), we will then frequently find ourselves letting up a little on the restrictive stuff and becoming a lot more laid-back and *Laissez-faire*. Sensing this change, our children will become a little more assertive, independent and perhaps "in charge." We then have some choices; we can move back to being more restrictive, but stay warm and fuzzy. Our children may then return to being compliant. Or we can withhold affection and distance ourselves somewhat emotionally, at which point our children may change from assertive to aggressive, from independent to rebellious and from well-adjusted to delinquent. Should we do both, that is, become more restrictive AND cold or distant, they may then withdraw and become sullen or quarrelsome.

## Management Differences

There is no law that states that you should be a management partner with someone who has exactly the same preferred style as yours. In fact, the opposite is likely to be true, as we have already noted. Therefore, your trainees will tend to behave quite differently for each of you, unless you are on a particularly good day where you are both on the same wavelength.

## Merged Companies

If you are a new manager in an already established company, you may need to recognize that it takes a very long time to establish a place at the warm, accepting end of the "feeling" dimension when you are taking on someone else's trainees. You are hooking up with someone who has perhaps had a lot of experience in this dimension and who has established a close relationship with the children. On the other hand, while the children may accept you as a person, they may not accept you as an authority figure, and you may therefore find yourself experiencing behaviours that are more in line with the Dismissive or Authoritarian style—even if YOU are ready to be accepting of these come-as-a-package children. It may therefore be prudent to put time into working on the acceptance dimension prior to becoming a part of the restrictive/permissive dimension. We take a look at general house rules you might be able to use in the meantime when we talk about Procedures later in the book.

## The Bottom Line

The bottom line here is that there is a very close relationship between our feelings and actions, and our children's feelings and actions. When we change, they change.

It is very important to note that changing your child's behaviour involves much more than simply tightening up on the rules, or moving along the permissive to restrictive dimension. You may end up moving from depressed to delinquent, and from rock to hard place. In fact, the most positive changes would seem to come from moving along the "feeling" dimension, from distant to close, from rejecting to accepting, from cold to warm. In reality, it is almost impossible to dictate how you want yourself to feel. It is, however, very important to remember that the more positive behaviours we want to see in our trainees are present in an atmosphere of acceptance—even if we can't quite manage the closeness and the warmth. Acceptance of an individual for who he is, warts and all, can be one of the most important factors in helping a family run smoothly.

## Management Training

Management *style* training is totally non-existent. You can take parenting courses, read parenting books, listen to advice from professionals, friends or relatives, but they tend to focus on ***techniques or strategies***, and ***different approaches*** to parenting that emanate from individuals who themselves have an established or preferred style. There is no doubt that these can be very helpful, and can certainly assist us in finding a style that fits our own way of being. In my experience, however, it seems that individuals only incorporate strategies that fit their own intrinsic style which reflects a unique blend of upbringing, personality and life experiences.

## The Sins of Our Fathers ...

Management style is built from genetics and learning, consciously or unconsciously, and different approaches are handed down from generation to generation, sometimes deliberately adopted, sometimes deliberately avoided. Don't forget your management consultants—those individuals who modelled parenting style for you. You have probably already recognized your own parents as Authoritarian or Authoritative, and recognized that each of your parents probably had a different style. You have probably also thought about some things that you do a certain way because your parents did them that way—or perhaps because your parents did NOT do them that way. I have frequently heard parents say "I swore I'd never raise my voice to my kids the way my old man did to me all the time," or "That's the way it was for us as kids, I don't see why it can't work for my children."

Unfortunately, we often tend to go to extremes in order to avoid the perceived "mistakes" of our parents. A child who NEVER hears a raised voice at home will find the outside world a very scary place to be, and may find it hard to judge which particular behaviours are more acceptable than others. If you are gently told "I really don't think that's a very nice thing to do" whether you are bothering your brother or robbing a bank, how are you supposed to tell which one is more significant? On the other hand, a child who ALWAYS hears raised voices at home will also have problems judging which particular behaviours are more acceptable than others. If you get yelled at just as loudly for accidentally spilling your juice as you do for setting fires in the middle of the living room, hey...what's the difference?

Being able to review our own upbringing is like looking in the rear-view mirror as we are driving along the road of life. We can see where we have been, with all the pitfalls that have been in our way, and with all the experiences we have had that have helped us choose the right turns in the road. This information may help us to understand how we have got to the place in the road where we find ourselves in the present. However, if we CONSTANTLY look in the rear-view mirror, especially if we focus only on ONE part of our previous experience as having positioned us where we are, we not only lose sight of the horizon ahead of us, but we also bump into a lot of obstacles (and people) on a daily basis.

YES, our parents have had a major influence on us, as we have a major influence on our children now. NO, they are not totally responsible for the choices we make, the road we travel or the direction in which we are headed. It is my firm belief (and the longer I am in the business of counselling, the stronger this belief) that parents make the best decisions that they can, given the information that they have at the time, in the best interests of their children as they understand them. This does not mean that, in the wisdom of hindsight, the decision was the one with the best outcome, or that even five seconds after a decision is made more information becomes available that might have resulted in a different decision. It does, however, mean that our parents made their parenting decisions in much the same way we do— in the midst of a particular cultural climate or media frenzy, with individual personalities and styles, and with specific information at hand.

## Individual Differences

Becoming the manager of a family company, fortunately or unfortunately, does not have much impact on a number of aspects of our basic personality. There are volumes written on individual differences and it has been fashionable from time to time to belong to a particular "type." We've all heard about "Type A" personalities with a high risk of heart disease and the "hippie/flower child" type with their laid-back, whatever-it-takes style. There are a myriad of personality "types," but for now we are just going to concentrate on a specific aspect of personality that I have found to be useful in helping families understand why there are conflicts in certain areas, and learn how to get the management model working again in spite of these. This particular approach is based on the psychological theories of Swiss psychologist Carl Jung concerning Extraversion and Introversion, and has a notable impact on interactions and decision making within families.

## Extraversion and Introversion

In brief, the major differences between those of us who are extraverts and those of us who are introverts is that extraverts find their sources of energy primarily from OUTSIDE themselves and introverts find their sources of energy primarily from INSIDE themselves. This generally means that extraverts need a social world of people in which they can find validation for their feelings and actions, while introverts tend to process their feelings and ideas very much internally, and therefore are not in constant need of external validation. Extraverts tend to express love, anger and other feelings outwardly, while introverts may withdraw and become passive in their hostility or inward in their love. Either way, introverts are harder to "read," while extraverts may bleed all over you, whether you want them to or not.

Some of the characteristics that describe these different personality types are adapted here from a book entitled *People Types and Tiger Stripes* by Gordon Lawrence:

| *EXTRAVERTS* | *INTROVERTS* |
|---|---|
| speak, then think | think, then speak |
| sociability | territoriality |
| interaction | concentration |
| external | internal |
| breadth | depth |
| extensive | intensive |
| multiple relationships | limited relationships |
| energy expenditure | energy conservation |
| external events | internal reactions |
| gregarious | reflective |

We have already flogged the dead horse of differences being just *different* and not *wrong*. However, one more blow is in order. The following possible combinations have very different outcomes, whether we are talking about management partners, or trainee combinations or management/ trainee relationships, since vastly different dynamics can be set up over very similar issues.

## Extraverts and Extraverts

When the individuals in a relationship (mom/dad, dad/child, mom/child, child/child) are both extraverts, a high degree of energy is expended out into the environment of the family. There will probably be a lot of open discussion and therefore probably a lot of open conflict. Both individuals will engage mouth then put brain in gear. There will thus be a lot of over-reaction and apologizing, a lot of giving and taking back, a lot of taking and giving back, as the thinking and problem solving are done out loud. Extraverts not only share most of what is in their minds, but also share it at the very beginning of the thinking process, expecting to have the ideas bounced right back from others, with some comments and opinions thrown in, so that they can then continue with their thinking process. Issues that cause conflict are therefore open and obvious, often with a lot of emotion thrown in, but are also over fairly quickly, since extraverts are not known for ruminating once the processing is over. Extraverts embrace change and variety, so do not tend to dwell on any one thing for too long. In fact, if life gets boring, they will often initiate change. Thus, the relationship between extraverts is constantly changing and frequently challenging to the other—creating more external energy upon which both tend to thrive. Extraverts tend to dominate family meetings, so extraverted trainees may seem to take over while introverted managers feel bulldozed. Sometimes the energy levels between extraverts become too high or exhausting or even dangerous, and they need a break from each other. Sometimes the competition between them for air time becomes too intense. Sometimes there is a lack of "sober second thought," and impulsive decisions or statements are made that may be difficult to take back or to change. Sometimes there is a lack of insight and introspection. A relationship between two extraverts can be a total mystery to more introverted types!

## Introverts and Introverts

Now we enter the mysterious world of mind reading and ESP. When two

introverts are in a relationship, there is a lot of inner processing and introspection going on that can provide each individual with a deep level of
commitment to and understanding of the other. Tremendous loyalties
develop, since introverts do not commit readily, and when they do they
expect similar commitment from the other individual. These inner loyalties
can be quite exclusive and not allow for diverse loyalties to others, leading
to possessiveness or feelings of jealousy that may be completely hidden
from the other partner. Sometimes the communication between two introverts is uncanny—they finish each others' sentences, they read each others' non-verbal cues, they "know" what the other wants without even
speaking. While this secret language may bind two introverts closely
together, it sometimes excludes (and unnerves!) everyone else. Introverts
often worry a lot about each other, although they may not let on. Introverts
frequently feel that other people are not the least interested in what they
are thinking or feeling, and therefore do not share these thoughts or feelings. If they do share, they share at the END of the process of thinking or
problem solving. Therefore, if there are joint management decisions to be
made or directions to be taken, it is frequently difficult for introverts to
talk them out with each other, because each one has thought it out before
they even start. Family or management meetings can be a real bust,
because introverts don't speak unless they have had the chance to think, or
unless someone specifically gives them a turn. Because introverts really do
not like change (which disrupts all kinds of established commitments and
loyalties), they are unlikely to initiate it. However, because they don't easily communicate what it is they don't like, there may be a lot of misunderstandings. Thus, relationships in families between introverts are likely to
be unspoken, but it is a mistake to believe that they are non-existent.

## Extraverts and Introverts

As we discussed earlier, we tend to pick partners who are quite different
from ourselves, and therefore a partnership between an extravert and an
introvert is not at all uncommon. Between them, they have all aspects of
this particular dimension, from being highly sociable to being capable of
deep introspection. For this partnership to work well, both partners need to
acknowledge that differences exist and that the other person does not
process the world in quite the same way. Introverts provide extraverts with
the opportunity to watch introspection in action and to see that sober sec-

ond thought before acting has its advantages. Extraverts, on the other hand, show introverts how to make small talk, how to handle spontaneous social situations and how to express feelings in words. Each will often settle upon letting the other partner do the work for which they are best suited. Provided this does not create problems for the relationship or the family, it is not a situation to be changed.

Unfortunately, for the most part, both extraverts and introverts believe that their partners think the same way they do. In other words, an extravert thinks that when an introvert says something, he has just that instant thought of it, and is throwing it out for comment, editing and discussion — because this is what the extravert would do. On the other hand, an introvert thinks that when an extravert says something, she has spent hours processing all the different aspects of the situation and has mind up her mind — because this is what the introvert would do.

The resulting exchange can thus go something like this:

## *Outward conversation:*

**Extravert:**   *How about we take the kids out for dinner tonight?*
(Inner thoughts: Hey, I just thought of this neat idea!)
(Feels: enthusiastic, ready to discuss possibilities.)

**Introvert:**   *Oh...okay.*
(Inner thoughts: I don't know why we always have to do everything her way.)
(Feels: resentful, dominated, ignored.)

**Outcome:**   Family goes out for dinner. The Extravert is reinforced for impulsive thinking and has a good time. She may feel guilty because there really isn't enough money for the family to keep eating out all the time, but surely the other manager would have said something if this was a problem, so it must be okay, so she tells herself she won't worry about it. The Introvert feels dragged along. He may have a good time, depending on everyone else, or he may get quite withdrawn and even sulky because the family really can't afford to keep eating out.

Here is another exchange.

## *Outward conversation:*

**Introvert:**  *How about we take the kids out for dinner tonight?*
(Inner thoughts:  I have thought about all the possibilities of what we could do for a meal tonight. I have thought about staying in, but have decided that I've done that for the past month and am fed up with doing all the cooking, so I figured we could either go out or order in. Then I decided that ordering in still means we have all the clearing up to do, and I'm fed up with nagging the kids to do the dishes. Even if we don't have a lot of money, we can probably scrape up enough to go to the little Italian place around the corner, and besides we all deserve a treat. Therefore, I have decided that going out for dinner is the best possible option.)

**Extravert:**  *Oh, I don't know about that; it's expensive. Why don't we order in?*
(Inner thoughts: This sounds like a good idea—but why don't I throw in another alternative and then we can bat a whole slew of different ideas around for a while!)

**Introvert:**  *Oh...okay.*
(Inner thoughts:  He is NEVER interested in what I want to do. I always have to do things his way. I guess he's thought about the hassles with the kids, but he doesn't care because I'm always the one who ends up doing the nagging. All he ever cares about is the money. Doesn't he know that I need a break, even if it does cost us?)

**Outcome:**  Family orders pizza. The kids make a mess. The Introvert fumes inside and glowers at the kids, and the kids don't clean up because no one has insisted they do so. The Extravert receives the reinforcement needed for continuing to think aloud. The Introvert is reinforced for thinking that no one cares, let alone does anything based on her input.

There have been a number of books written about the tendency for males and females to misinterpret what the other is saying, notably Deborah Tannen's *You Just Don't Understand* and John Gray's *Men Are From Mars, Women Are From Venus*. These authors put a number of different viewpoints and bodies of research together to provide an additional perspective on communication between individuals. Add these viewpoints to the extraversion/introversion issues, and it doesn't take a rocket scientist to see why there are so many conflicts of communication within family companies.

## Trainee Issues

When a company has a good mix of extraverts and introverts, all the various communication patterns surface and there is exposure to all permutations. Even if this leads to misunderstandings and conflict, usually everyone is aware of the dynamics and differences that can occur.

It can be quite different, however, if the management partners are the same type, but one of the trainees is different. An extraverted child born to two introverted parents can be not only an enigma but a worry. This situation becomes worse in some respects if all other siblings are the same type as the parents, since the child who is different will really stand out. However, if it is a single child family, the child is QUITE likely to be seen as being in charge, simply because he is more vocal and tends to bulldoze through issues with his parents. These children are likely to end up in my office for help with "anger management" because all family members are bewildered by this child's open emotions. In addition, parents are frequently seduced into trying to resolve situations initiated by the child's dramatic cry of "I'll NEVER be able to do this!" or "I have NO friends!" or "You are ALWAYS so mean!" since the child (in the eyes of his parents) has obviously thought this all through and has come to a well-founded conclusion.

*Annie was an attractive, vivacious eight-year-old young lady who was brought in by her parents because they felt she might be hyperactive. She was the eldest of three children, quite bright, achieving well in school. Dad was a research scientist, Mom a librarian. The other two children were quiet and shy, preferring solitary activities or board games to any kind of noisy or*

*boisterous play. Annie, on the other hand, reveled in high levels of activity; she liked to play on the climber, engage in a form of tackle football with the neighbourhood boys, and be outside in all types of weather with her friends. She seemed to need to let off steam when she got home from school, complaining that Mrs. Noble made them sit in their seats all day long and that they were NEVER allowed to talk in class. At home, her parents reported that she wanted to talk nonstop and that she dominated the conversation at mealtimes. In the office, she was very polite, allowing her parents to speak and only responding when spoken to. She made good eye contact, and was content to be part of the adult conversation, listening intently when her parents were talking. When excused to the waiting room, she spent her time colouring and reading the various magazines and books.*

*Information from Mom and Dad revealed that they had both been brought up in very quiet, well-disciplined households where introversion was clearly a characteristic that was valued. In Mom's family, mealtimes were completely silent because her father had insisted on it. Dad was the only child of shy parents, and the bulk of conversations had been discussions of books or current events. Neither parent had been encouraged to join sports teams or partake in physical activities, and both had been enthusiastic about books from a very early age. Currently, they listed their favourite activities as reading, gardening and spending quiet time. Their other two children participated in and enjoyed these activities, whereas Annie was always quite reluctant to spend more than a few minutes on such pursuits, grumbling all the time that she wanted to be with her friends.*

*There was little "wrong" in this family except the need to understand and adapt to Annie's extraversion. She craved social interaction as much as the others craved peace; she expressed her opinions and feelings as much as the others hid theirs; and she had a clear need for exchanging energy with her environment. Once we explored this as being quite normal—different but not wrong—and manageable if they accepted her, rather than trying to change her, things settled down in terms of the level of parental anxiety. Annie will probably always be the source of some discomfort in this low-key household, and she may always be tempted to look outside the family for her validation.*

If an introverted child is born into a family of extraverts, this child is likely to end up in a counsellor's office for help with "depression" or with "difficulties with social relationships." Extraverted managers worry endlessly about trainees who withdraw, who keep their thoughts to themselves, who are hard to "read," and who say "nothing" whenever they are asked what is bothering them. Many such parents reluctantly admit that their worst fear is that this child will end up withdrawing completely from the world, never have any friends, and be totally isolated from society. Introverted trainees may simply not feel ready to share, not yet know exactly what words they want to use, or have not found quite the right time to say something. Extraverted parents tend to pursue introverted children in an effort to get them to externalize their thinking. These parents are often "blown away" by the child's sudden explosion when they can't take any more interference or there is nowhere else to hide. Introverted children often prefer their own company to the company of others, especially if they have spent the vast part of their waking day in group situations—at a caregiver's, nursery school, elementary or high school, participating in family activities, and so on. This is frequently enough social contact for them; now they need their thinking time.

This is not to say that withdrawal or outbursts of anger are always normal or fine; to extremes, either can certainly be cause for concern and a reason to run a reality check by a professional. Even if a particular behaviour pattern or response style is normal for a particular individual, it can still cause tremendous problems within the family company, and everyone may need some assistance to restore the balance. Learning to understand the patterns or response styles by understanding various aspects of personality can, however, be very useful in predicting and therefore controlling a wide variety of day-to-day situations and conflicts.

## And the Moral of This Story is ...

We have seen that there are a number of different factors that influence parental style, and that children not only tolerate but in fact adapt to a wide variety of approaches during our learning process as family managers. Most of us tend to overparent our firstborn (they certainly are exposed to all of our mistakes) and are then surprised to find that what worked with the firstborn for sure will NOT work with the second one, so we have to make mistakes all over again. By the time the third one comes along, if we are so inclined, we have usually given up trying to find one way and one way only. We tend to be much more relaxed as parents, even to the point of what I like to call benign neglect, since by this time we have discovered that there really is not a right way to do it, so we might as well take things as they come, and attempt to manage in a way that provides a good quality of life within the family unit. However, this does not mean that we give up completely; children have to be parented, trainees have to be trained.

So what can we do, then, to try to get some logic, order and structure into our families? Whatever it is, however we do it, it has somehow to be independent of the various personalities and styles, and we have to stop looking for what it right and what is wrong. The next chapters explore the ideas of Policies and Procedures, as a way of providing a framework within which many different personalities and parenting philosophies can fit. This is not an attempt to tell you WHAT to do, but instead explore how you might be able to organize your own goals for your own company, so that your trainees get the messages you want them to get and receive the training you know they need in order to develop their own management style and attain the skills required to start companies of their own.

# 5

# Family Policies

All businesses have policies that guide their direction and their purpose. Family companies are no different. Family policies are rooted in the basic value systems by which we live our lives as human beings. These are the "big picture" issues which provide a total context within which day-to-day decisions are made.

> Policies may differ from one company to another, since no two families have identical value systems, and we may not always agree with those that are different from our own. Nevertheless, they are different, not right or wrong. No company can dictate to another company what its value systems should or should not be.

> Having a value system, whatever it may be, and living by it is generally preferable to having no value system at all or, worse, not even seeing the need to have one.

## Traditional Sources of Policy

Traditionally, and currently in many households, policies were set by outside organizations and influences. Various religions have definite and strong policies concerning how life should be lived, and families over the years have taken and used these policies to guide family decisions. "Do unto others as you would have them do unto you," for example, dictates many procedures around personal interactions and standards regarding respect for privacy and for property. A policy based on religious grounds can be backed up by promises of eternal peace for adherence, or assurance of damnation for failure to comply. Reasons given to children may include "because God says so," "because it says so in the Bible," "because that's what Rabbi Cohen says"—and so on. These sources are pretty compelling and very comforting for parents to have as a back-up for management decisions. Even those who claim to be without religious beliefs may have a hard time contemplating the possibility of eternal damnation.

A similar source of values comes from our own cultural heritage, be it Western or Eastern in philosophy, native or imported, or even local or regional in geography. Various ethnic groups have practices rooted in tradition or folklore that are frequently non-negotiable for members of the particular group, and are therefore taken for granted.

Policies generated from any or all of these traditional sources will normally work very well until the trainees start to become aware of alternative viewpoints—usually in young adolescence—and begin to question and challenge religious beliefs, frequently in a determined and persistent manner. This is not particularly because they want them to change or for us to change, but simply because challenging management practices is what trainees need to do in order to develop eventual policies of their own. "But we've always done it that way!" doesn't usually cut much ice with trainees who, in the absence of factual information and experience, can frequently see endless possibilities for doing things differently.

## Parent Company Values

Another traditional source of values, of course, has been our original family company. We are all aware of the messages we grew up with from our own parents. "Children should be seen and not heard," "A woman's place is in the home," "Respect your elders," "A bird in the hand is worth two in the bush," and so on, may all ring familiar bells. Some of us may have grown up with the messages, "Whatever Dad says goes... or else," "Don't tell anyone what goes on in our family," "Do as you are told when you are told." Once we are managers in our own companies, what sometimes happens is that we deliberately take a stand on messages we have been taught either by refusing ever to treat our children the way we were treated, or by subscribing to the notion that if it was good enough for us it will be good enough for them. As with most things in life, all or nothing is seldom the best compromise.

## Media Influence

As the influence of traditional religions has diminished, the growth and power of another source of policies has become somewhat overwhelming. The mass media have taken over as a major source of information regarding human behaviour and thus exert a major influence over management decisions of today. We learn not only from what the media say, but also from what they do. While this is certainly not all negative since it opens up a much wider variety of choices in terms of alternative lifestyles and standards, we need to be alert to some of the more subtle messages that may influence our policy decisions. Some examples would be: "It is cool to drink and smoke," "Violence doesn't really hurt; they are only acting," "Violence is happening everywhere, so it is inevitable," "People who make policies are not to be trusted," "Just because you are guilty does not mean you have to pay for what you did," "Things are important only as long as they make headlines," "Human misery is everywhere," "Good news does not get reported," "Women are thin and beautiful," "Men are strong and macho," "You cannot expect to be employed," "Whatever happens, sue, and if you don't win, appeal"... you get the picture.

## Current Management Practices

It is vital that we, as managers of our own company, be as aware as humanly possible of the policies our trainees are picking up and internalizing from whatever source—and, even more important, that we NEVER underestimate our own influence in this process. Remember how influenced you have been by your parent company values, and *your* parents thought you weren't listening! Even if our children spend infinitely more hours tuned in to media values than they do listening to ours, our influence is still potentially stronger. Whether they appear to be or not, they are listening and, above all, watching to see what our policies are, whether they are consistent, and how strongly we are prepared to defend them.

In the early stages of discussion with our partner as to whether or not we are going to form a company, we normally do not spend an inordinate amount of time together discussing future policies regarding trainee issues such as homework, teenage birth control, hours per week of television viewing, or number of pierces permissible in which body parts. Partners who decide to commit to company formation may well sense or know (or think they know) at least some of the other's value systems, and in fact we do tend to be attracted to those who appear to have similar philosophies of life. Sometimes we turn out to be mistaken, and often company breakups are due to major policy differences.

Policy formation and review is an ongoing task of the family company. New situations call for a review of the status quo and sometimes for a new policy. In response to a crisis, temporary procedures may need to be put into place to handle damage control; however immediate policy change without due consideration and consultation is unwise. There is no question that policy changes are made only by management, although clearly trainees' perspectives, opinions and/or suggestions are important information to be considered in the process.

## Conflicting Policies

There can be contradictory policies even in the most harmonious, consensual households. "In this family, honesty is essential" and "In this family, we care about people's feelings" are two policies that would happily co-exist in most families. However, when one of the trainees is given an expensive but totally inappropriate, ugly or useless present by a valued consultant, the two policies may be in direct opposition! Rock—trainee—hard place. It may be necessary to explain to trainees that there can be exceptions to what seem to be solid, consistent policies, and that in some situations, one particular policy takes precedence over the other. There is no easy way out of this one; that's life.

For managers, the policy most likely to cause trouble is the one stating, "We strive to keep our trainees happy"—since this will be at odds with other noble values such as "Education is important," "We all contribute to the good of the family," "We share," "We show appreciation for things that others do," and so on.

There will be difficulties for trainees if management partners do not agree on policy. This happens in intact companies as well as in restructured companies. Single manager companies do not have the same in-house conflict as do partnerships, but there is frequently inconsistency for the trainees who hop from one company to another. It has, however, been my experience that, despite huge conflict and apparently opposing views on procedures and style, parent partners, even if separated, are not necessarily at odds over "policy." They frequently agree that education is important, or that necessities come before luxuries; they *disagree* on just how to achieve these goals. Within intact partnerships, it is important to work for consensus on policy, even if there has to be some compromise to do so, since this is in the best interests of the trainees. It is hard to work with one manager believing that you "turn the other cheek," while the other is firmly committed to "an eye for an eye."

Children are sometimes amazingly adaptable, and may learn to live with the confusion of conflicting policies if they have no choice. What they will do, however, is manipulate the contradictory positions to their own ends, using whichever one suits the current purpose. This may turn them into even more devious creatures than they already are! Chronic family conflict may result, and the management/trainee hierarchy will be threatened since the ability to manipulate management in this way provides children with more power than is appropriate to maintain the balance.

## Unpredictability

Perhaps the most confusing situation for a trainee is when there is inconsistency of policy *within the same manager*. Unpredictability is scary. Alcoholic or substance-abusing parents are unpredictable, as are depressed or stressed parents. While it can occasionally be to management's advantage to act unpredictably, especially if a change is needed in a negative behaviour pattern, as an ongoing behaviour it is a major source of anxiety to trainees. A manager acting predictably enables trainees to learn how to respond appropriately, to become comfortable with their limits, to feel a healthy sense of control over their environment, and generally to increase their level of security.

## Six General Policy Areas

Although each company has its own individual needs, there are six general policy areas in which management plays a major role over a period of many years:   safety, health, education, spiritual values, financial policies and mutual respect.

**Safety** of trainees is usually paramount in families. Think about it. In even the most democratic family, you would have no hesitation whatsoever in grabbing your child, hard if necessary, to prevent him from running across a busy street, whether he wanted you to or not. "In this family, we place safety first and foremost" is a widespread policy. Knowing where an older teen is going and when she will be home is an extension of this safety policy that can continue to be of concern to management, even after trainees have left to start their own companies. Sources of much conflict between managers and trainees can be the misperception on the part of trainees that management concerns over safety reflect a high level of control over freedom, and the misperception on the part of managers that most control issues can be packaged as "safety" issues.

**Health** of trainees is also high on the list of the priorities for family policies. This usually encompasses such areas as nutrition, fitness and related lifestyle choices. Although not as difficult as the safety issue for parents to relinquish, trainees frequently battle to take control in the area of health policy, at least once they reach adolescence. If established early in the life of the company and modelled as well as preached by management, health policy can become a given, particularly when it is reinforced through the education system. However, there will be a time when trainees visit other companies and see other lifestyle choices that seem to be more fun and less hassle, and there may be much pressure on health policy issues at that time.

**Education**, in terms of school-related issues, is another global area in which management frequently takes and retains a leadership role throughout the training period. For the most part, other than "education takes a high priority in this family," general family values—"a job worth doing is worth doing well," "finish what you start," and "necessities first, luxuries later"—are applicable and helpful when it comes to school. However, within the broad area of education, there are many issues in which trainees take control, usually because "you can take a horse to water but you can't make him drink." For example, even if parents chain children to their desks and put them on bread-and-water-only rations, it is impossible to mandate learning. In families where the policy is "success at all costs," parents are frequently so determined to have children make it through school successfully that they take over far too many of the trainee-type duties, sometimes to the point where they become the child's memory, planner, project organizer, typist and general production assistant. The problem is that there is only so much work to be done. The more work that is taken over by the manager, who of course already knows how to do this and probably does it quite well, the less room there is for the trainee to learn by experience. This experience, so necessary for proper and healthy growth, includes learning from mistakes and less-than-perfect attempts to complete tasks.

Once again, if education policies are established early and procedures put into place, the entire system becomes part of the routine of the family, and there may be few if any problems for families in this area.

**Spiritual values** may stem from a family's religious upbringing or they may simply come from an idiosyncratic sense of a bigger picture or higher power. One of the risks of interfaith marriages is the potential for a clash of values between management partners, with such differences occurring at the level of tradition, ritual or basic underlying belief system. Children tend to learn their spiritual values from the way their parents live, rather than from what their parents say. Again, during adolescence, it is a trainee's job to question spiritual values in order to validate beliefs, to solidify areas that have been in doubt and to try out new directions in order to see whether they satisfy curiosity and bring comfort. Many managers take it personally if trainees question such basics as spirituality; however, it is an integral part of the training program.

**Financial policies** are much more symbolic and important than they may at first appear. Money is power. With the possible exception of disagreements about trainees, management partners fight more often about money than any other issue, whether or not they have children. Policies brought into the family company by the individual managers may well differ significantly, from "take care of the pennies, and the pounds will take care of themselves" to "spend what you have; life is too short." The undeniable fact for trainees, however, is that money buys independence, and so they must remain dependent upon their parent company and thus under parental control until they are able to support themselves financially. Parental financial policies are therefore of considerable interest to trainees pretty much from the time they can articulate the words "mine!" and "more!"

**Mutual respect** encompasses a broad range of policies and values relating to respect for self and others, including individuals, groups and property. Policies in this area include those that govern: general manners and company etiquette; ways of interacting with people, including authority figures; family rituals, such as gift-giving, behaviour with older generations, expectations regarding visitations; respect for property belonging to self and others; personal hygiene; and maintenance of company premises. What is of great interest in this particular policy area is that people outside the family company may become aware of your trainee's expertise before you do. How many of us have craned our necks at a parent-teacher interview to make sure that the teacher is in fact talking about our child? Or checked the name at the top of the report card? Or asked neighbours or friends, "You mean OUR Jennifer?" It is always important to pat yourself on the back when you hear how wonderful your child is to everyone else, even though you are utterly astounded, and are now more convinced than ever that your trainee indeed must hate you. The fact that they can apply your policies appropriately indicates that they have been well trained.

## Leaving the Nest

Fortunately, as managers, we are not the only source of potential value systems for our trainees. During the course of their training program, they will be exposed to a huge range of differing policies, among which they must sift and pick and choose those that will eventually become part of their own unique mosaic. We tend to worry deeply when our children seem to adopt value systems as readily as a chameleon takes on its background colour, particularly during young adolescence when trying on values seems to occur along with trying on clothes. Research tells us that adolescents look to their peers for "today" values such as clothing, music, idols, language and general appearance, but that they tend to stick closer to parental values for longer-term issues such as spirituality, education and future-oriented goals. Hang in.

One of the primary indicators that a trainee is ready to be independent is that she is capable of keeping herself safe, healthy and independent in a wide range of circumstances by having developed a set of guidelines or policies of her own. While these may, and arguably perhaps should, be somewhat different from the policies of the parent company, they serve to provide a set of values by which the trainee lives her life. It is a new experience for most older teens and young adults to be faced with no set of rules to break other than their own.

## A Tale of Two Families —Policies at Work

Since there are no "right" or "wrong" policies as such, and different policies can produce similar results in terms of a child's ability to respond in a wide variety of circumstances, the best illustration of the effect policies can have is to compare two completely different individuals, evidencing similar problems. We can then attempt to see how the family philosophies got them where they were *and* how they got them out of it.

Both families initially appeared to be very similar from many perspectives, and both presented issues that are not the least uncommon for companies with older teenagers as trainees.

 *Lisa and Katie were both 18 years old when we first met. Both had been dragged into therapy by their mothers because life at home was becoming unbearable. They were both alternately charming and obnoxious—the former when they wanted something, the latter when denied it. Anger was a huge issue in both households, with each girl engaging in sound-and-light shows that sent other siblings scurrying for cover and left both parents bewildered. Both girls came from middle-class family backgrounds, Lisa being the youngest of three girls, with her next oldest sister still living at home, and Katie the younger of two, with an older brother living several hundred miles away. Both were doing reasonably well in school. Lisa was bright, on the point of leaving school to go to university and planning to be a physiotherapist. Katie was pretty average and her marks reflected this. She did not yet know what she wanted to do when she left school. Both girls had dads who were relatively uninvolved in the family. Lisa's dad was a very busy financial officer in a company that was undergoing extensive downsizing, and he spent most waking moments at work or in front of his computer. Katie's dad was also a very busy man, openly stressed by work, also affected by downsizing in that his workload had doubled and his staff had been halved. Both men earned reasonable salaries, and lack of finances was not a major issue in either family. Lisa occasionally met her*

*dad for lunch, while Katie enjoyed breakfast out with her dad every weekend. Both families tried to make a point of having at least Sunday dinner together.*

*Although Lisa's mom worked full-time at home as a homemaker and Katie's mom worked full-time outside the home as a secretary, both women saw themselves as the executive director of the family and confided that they felt very guilty and responsible if household chores were not done perfectly. Both girls had a list of expectations to fulfill around the house, including responsibility for homework, chores, belongings and room. According to both, however, they were expected to do far more than their siblings had ever been required to do. Many of the outbursts were triggered by this perception of unfairness and by their mothers' nagging when the chores were not done to their satisfaction or when the girls broke various house rules.*

*All members of each family were deeply unhappy and wanted many things changed. Both girls were equally adamant that THEY wanted to change things by leaving home. There was no argument from either of them that life at home was the pits—constant fighting, blaming, nagging, resentment...and then it was time for breakfast! Lisa desperately wanted to go away to university; Katie wanted to move in with a friend downtown and finish school from there.*

But here the similarities ended. Both girls came from families with vastly different family policies, and these had had quite an impact on the development of value systems in each teen, as well as on the degree to which each girl had established her independence from the family and her readiness to leave the parent company to start managing alone.

## Lisa

 *Discussions with Mom (Dad was always "too busy" to come to appointments) indicated that Lisa had been raised with the following family policies, which were articulated with little or no prompting:*

*In this family, we believe that everyone is responsible for his or her own belongings.*

*In this family, we believe that health and education are important.*
*In this family, we believe in a strong work ethic.*
*In this family, accountability accompanies responsibility.*
*In this family, life is not always fair.*
*In this family, family time is important, even if it*
  *occurs infrequently.*

There were endless "procedures"—rules about everything
from curfews to how to stack the dishes properly in the dishwash-
er, each with a rationale that was attached to one or other policy
—but Mom complained that she no longer had a means of making
the girls abide by ANY of these procedures, and that she was constantly threatening dire consequences that she could no longer
follow through. We talked a little about Mom's anticipatory grief
when both Tanya and Lisa finally left home, and even a little
about Mom's fear that Dad might disappear at the same time , but
Mom maintained that she had not come to talk about herself or
her relationship—we were here to deal with Lisa's anger.

When I questioned Lisa about her OWN rules (the expectations she had of herself that would become the policies in her own
company) she was able to state them clearly and unambiguously.
She was a non-smoker and did not do drugs ("I believe in keeping
my body healthy"), and a social drinker ("I drink in moderation
except when I know I'll be driving home and then I don't drink at
all"), and quite capable of keeping herself safe ("I don't get in a
car with anyone who has been drinking"; "I engage only in safe
sex and only then within a committed relationship"; "I always
carry a quarter for the phone and a $20 bill for a taxi"). She had
a solid circle of friends that consisted of some she had known
since she was in Kindergarten, and an extended family about
whom she talked with pride and affection. It was fairly obvious
that Lisa was quite ready to leave home, but she reported that
Mom had said she would have to attend university in her own
hometown because they could not afford to pay for her to live
away. Lisa said that she had quite a bit of money saved, enough to
support her fully for her first year of university, and that she
planned to continue to work her way through school. Because of
the family's policies, she had learned how to look after herself and
had become capable of a high level of independence. We talked a

*great deal about the fact that she seemed to have some good points to make, but that she tended to lose them in the middle of her rages. We practised some assertiveness, rather than aggressiveness, in putting these points across at home.*

*In Lisa's case, the main issue at the root of the family's unhappiness appeared to have more to do with getting ready to let go, rather than not being ready to leave. With some support, Lisa was able to reassure her mom that she would manage fine, and that leaving did not mean leaving for good. She was also able to share some of her very real anxieties about living away from home (just because she wanted to go did not mean she was one hundred per cent ready) and both Mom and Lisa were able to recognize that some of the outbursts were actually rooted in this anxiety. We were able to look fairly realistically at the "rules" and reduce them to a minimum set that revolved around natural consequences and Mom not supporting or condoning any activities of which she did not approve. We also worked on what were "commands" and what was "advice," and managed to practise making the switch. Lisa and Mom together were able to negotiate around some of the rules, and Mom was able to stop nagging somewhat once she realized that Lisa had in fact heard and acknowledged her advice, even if she didn't always take it. Mom still became highly agitated at the "threat" of Lisa leaving home, and the last time I saw them, the matter had not been settled. Mom's unwillingness or lack of readiness to deal with any of her own issues meant that the situation at home did not improve totally, and they did not come back for any more sessions.*

## Katie

*Katie's mom and dad were both present for the discussion of family policies, and had some considerable trouble deciding what they were, occasionally becoming quite heated with each other. When I tried to summarize and reflect what I felt they were trying to say, they would both look at me quite puzzled and politely indicate that I did not know what I was talking about. In the end, they went away from the session with a promise to come back next time having thought about what their policies were in several key areas so*

*that we could start to take a look at the context in which the family operated.*

*Mom came alone to the next session, somewhat embarrassed about the fact that Dad had said that he thought that this therapy "crap" was for the birds. Hadn't they come to fix Katie's problems and there they were talking to each other! However, she had persisted with the "homework" and came prepared with a list that, after some further clarification, boiled down to the following:*

*In this family, I try at all times to keep everyone happy.*

*This policy was attempted with every good intention. Mom was a kind, considerate, hard-working woman who was very much in love with her husband, and who was trying very hard to love her children. Both children, Katie from within the house and brother Seth from the other end of the province, had become constantly demanding, of everything from money to time and attention. The message to Mom and Dad always seemed to be "if you don't give it to me, or do it for me, I'll be unhappy." This threat, however veiled, sent both of them into orbits of increasing guilt and produced money, time and attention. When Seth came home, he and Katie spent the vast majority of their time together fighting over who could get and keep parental attention the longest, or calculating to the penny who had outdone whom in terms of money, whereupon the "loser" went screeching for justice. Katie was not happy when asked to do chores, to keep her room relatively tidy, to come home at certain times (or at all), to introduce her parents to her various boyfriends of which she had quite a list, to be accountable for her choices—in fact, she was not happy at all. This unhappiness had reached such proportions that she spent hardly any time at home, which you might think would have suited everyone fine, except in fact it suited no one.*

*When asked about her OWN rules, Katie stared at me as if I'd suddenly spoken to her in Chinese. It took several tries to explain to her what I meant about having rules that govern how we ourselves behave, and I had to give her some simple examples of what other teens had shared with me before she could even begin to formulate her own. She clearly had little idea of healthy lifestyle choices ("I smoke when I want to, when I can get ciga-*

*rettes, and I smoke as much as I want." "I don't drink at home, I only drink when I'm out with my friends") and equally little idea of keeping herself safe ("If I'm driving, I'll stop drinking when I start to feel drunk"; "If the driver's been drinking, that's not MY responsibility, it's his car and his licence!"). Her rules around sexual activity were interesting. "I'll only sleep with someone I know" and "I always leave it up to the guy to make sure he has a condom," seemed to be the main ones—and both of these she seemed to be breaking with regularity, frequently waking up in bed with an individual she barely remembered, let alone remembering whether or not they had used a condom. When this apparent breaking of her own rules was reflected to her, she looked puzzled and then said: "Oh, no, you've got it all wrong; I'd known the guy the whole evening! I didn't even DANCE with anyone else! And he seemed like a really responsible sort of person."*

*The ensuing process of working with Mom and Dad to try to establish policies at home was rather dismal. Twenty-five years into the life of the company is a little on the late side to start. It turned out that they had quite different views on what the policies should in fact be, and this, of course, complicated the process to the point where they gave up. It was not possible for Katie (or me, for that matter) to reassure Mom that she was indeed able to keep herself safe, and this perpetuated Mom's compulsion to take care of her. When Mom realized what messages the children had received (notably, "We are entitled to have you make us happy at all times" and "You are not being a good mother if you don't make us happy"), she began to feel quite depressed, since these were not the messages she had intended to send. I pointed out that, although it was a little hard to do, she could try to take back these messages and replace them with ones that would be more useful to the children as they tried to cope with the real world outside the family.*

*Mom has tried valiantly to take a stand on a number of issues, notably those involving her time, effort and money, and has also made a stab at letting some natural consequences take their course for Katie. Dad, unfortunately, continues as he had before, blustering a lot but ending up forking over cash to keep the kids quiet. Mom's "stand" tends to falter in the face of this industrial sabotage. Mom and Katie have worked somewhat at trying to make life at home a little more tolerable—with some limited suc-cess—but the deep unhappiness at home has not really shifted since they primarily try to avoid or ignore each other. Mom and Dad's relationship seems to remain solid, and they long for the day that Katie leaves home. At this point in time, however, Katie is still there, always meaning to save up enough money to leave, and threatening to do so at any moment, especially when things do not go her way. She is involved in a "long-term, committed relation-ship" that has so far lasted three weeks. While she seems to real-ize the need to live by a set of rules, she still finds it easier to change the rules quite frequently to fit her behaviour than to stick with a particular value system. This makes her happy, she says.*

# 6

# From Policy to Procedures

Procedures are the means by which policies are applied in the real world—the "letter of the law" that can be stated in concrete terms and monitored in a more direct manner. Procedures are defined as the *rules and expectations* that evolve from company policy and are specifically designed to operationalize the policies; in other words, they make them work. They guide behaviour in given situations, based on the overall direction decided upon by the management of the company. Some procedures are negotiable, some are not. Lord, grant us the wisdom to know the difference.

Some families seems to manage with policies alone, but this is rare, with the possible exception of spiritual values. Occasionally, providing a policy and encouraging family members to use their own judgment can work, especially as trainees become more experienced and competent, and as particular policies become ways of life for all concerned. For example, a general policy might be: "In this family, we do not believe in violence," and everyone in the family may well be able to govern his or her specific behaviour in given situations simply by remembering that this is the general policy, without having to have a specific rule about hitting. Generally speaking, however, policies are too vague, general and indirect to be helpful in individual situations or with specific issues, especially when children are young and inexperienced as trainees.

Most of us who have worked for large corporations or institutions are familiar with the procedural manuals that accompany major policy decisions, with the rules and regulations whose formulation keeps entire departments of administrators employed. Many of us have also felt our judgment, initiative and creativity stymied and our hands tied by rules governing everything from accounting procedures to when we need thirteen duplicate copies. Some of us are born to love procedures; they give us security. Some of us fight them constantly; they give us claustrophobia. When children are still young trainees, they frequently do not have what it takes to implement general policies without some guidelines as to how to do this. Neither do they have the knowledge or experience to "know" what these procedures should be without clear direction and guidance.

***There is no question that children cannot function without clear limits,*** whether these limits can be gently suggested or whether they must be firmly imposed. Thus, the formulation of appropriate procedures that are in line with general policy is critical in the management of the family and in the job of training children to be managers themselves one day.

The major rationale for having procedures and guidelines for children is that they need to be able to make their OWN rules which will govern their own lives once they are beyond the confines of their original family company. Breaking other people's rules is one thing, breaking your own is entirely another. Thus, our job as managers is to teach the trainees how to set and uphold procedures so that they can accept responsibility and privilege, and so that they can be in charge of their own behaviour by learning to be accountable. (Another reason we have rules in families is that anarchy works even less well than democracy, and often trainees confuse the two concepts.)

There are two main types of procedures: general operating procedures or house rules; and individual job descriptions.

## General Operating Procedures—or House Rules

General operating procedures apply to everyone in the family company, including visiting trainees, management consultants, temporary lodgers and even casual visitors. These procedures govern general behaviour on company property and help people know what is expected of them, regardless of position. They tend to fall into one of several main categories, the most important and universal being SAFETY/HEALTH and MUTUAL RESPECT. As a rule of thumb, using the word "when" makes a house rule sound a lot less like a threat and much more like a statement of fact. The use of the word "please" also helps. Examples of house rules that apply to EVERYONE, along with their policy category, might be:

## Safety/Health:

Fingers and other body parts are not to be placed in electrical outlets.

Operating machinery is done without supervision only by those who have appropriate knowledge and expertise.

This house is a non-smoking environment.

Seatbelts are required to be fastened at all times in the car.

Bicycles operate only when accompanied by bicycle helmets.

When you are last in, please lock up.

When you are the last to leave, please lock up.

When you are going to be later than expected, please inform someone in the company.

When you go out, please let someone know where you are going and what time you will be home.

## Mutual Respect:

When you wish to borrow something from someone, ask permission and be sure to return it when you are finished.

When you have plans that involve any other member(s) of the family, such as being driven somewhere or borrowing the family car, be sure to inform with reasonable notice.

When you do not plan to be home for a particular meal, inform the cook.

Swearing means 25 cents in the "Swear Jar" ($1 for adults).

Leave the toilet seat down.

Flush.

When you make the mess, you clean it up.

Stay at the table until everyone else is finished.

Incoming telephone calls are permitted between the hours of 7 a.m. and 10 p.m. only, unless it is a true emergency.

When a door is closed, please knock and wait for a reply before entering.

When you have finished using the lights, please turn them off.

When you use the car, please put gas in it.

When you notice the supply of something is running low, let management know—and please don't take the last one unless you have checked that it's okay to do so.

When you leave something in common family areas, it may be used and/or removed by others.

**Reminders:** Any member of the company may remind any other member about general operating rules, since they apply to everyone. This is especially helpful in blended or step families, since none of the above qualifies as a "parenting" responsibility, but rather as a living-in-harmony necessity. A polite reminder, using an appropriate tone of voice, along with appropriate timing and the almost mandatory use of the word "please," will frequently influence the success of this intervention as well as provide a good training opportunity for the children. It is not, however, up to trainees to "police" other trainees, management consultants or visitors in the event of procedural violations, since the responsibility for ensuring compliance ultimately rests with management.

When a family is restructured, there are often conflicts over who is in charge of whom and what rules apply where and when. The concept of general operating rules works well in such situations, since no single child has to "belong" to a particular parent in order for these procedures to apply, and there does not have to be any particular territoriality with respect to whose managerial responsibility it is for the application of the house rule. They also work well as trainees become increasingly independent, less like children and more like roommates. In fact, over time, house rules become habits. If you live in a blended family, you can often ascertain if a particular situation you are dealing with is a "house rule" or a "parenting" issue by asking yourself the question: "Would I be saying it this way if this person were my roommate?" If the answer is "yes," then it's not a parenting issue. If the answer is "no," it may be, and thus the person responsible for dealing with the particular situation may well be the child's own biological parent.

## What's Good for the Goose...

There are often conflicts in families over whether procedures apply to adults as well as children. In fact, there are frequently situations where rules clearly apply only to one or the other—sometimes to one child and not another, sometimes to adults not to children, sometimes vice versa. In a company, for example, management generally has access to certain privileges that are not readily available to Joe Trainee: expense accounts, executive washroom, additional benefit packages, nicer furnishings, and so on. In addition, society has definite rules about the age at which an individual can be licensed to drive a car, when it is legal to smoke and drink, when you are considered to be responsible for your debts, and so on. Family life is not always that clear-cut.

Families have basically two choices in situations where they expect different behaviours, responsibilities or privileges for different individuals.

**Choice No. 1** is to have one rule, expectation or procedure and to turn a blind eye to, or defend, those individuals who are permitted to break it. For example, if there is a general policy and procedure regarding violence or lack thereof, Dad may be allowed to restrain, or siblings may be allowed to "play" fight, whereas you are not permitted to punch out your younger brother or sister. In these circumstances, someone, sooner or later, has to do a LOT of explaining to everyone else who is and is NOT allowed to use physical violence and why or why not. Everyone ends up very confused and resentful, with the rule tending to get broken again and again while everyone tries to establish each new situation as a possible exception. The positive aspect here is that, if and when everyone DOES abide by the procedure, life runs peacefully and smoothly, and thus having one rule for everyone, with no exceptions tolerated, can be the optimal choice. The fact of life is, however, that there are definitely situations where it is totally *inappropriate* for children to live by the same rules as adults, or adults to live by the same rules as children. This is one of the main reasons why children can have a distorted view of their place within the family. Problems inevitably arise if children have inappropriate expectations regarding life outside the family, and expect nursery school teachers, day-care providers, other parents and all authority figures to allow them to have adult-type limits in the real world.

**Choice No. 2** is to have as many different rules or expectations as you need to suit each individual. For example, adults may be allowed to drink alcohol in the house, children may not. Older children may be allowed to stay up later than younger children. Adults may be permitted to spank, children may not hit. The main problem with this choice is that trainees will complain that "It's not FAIR!" The primary and necessary response to this complaint has to be "You are right—it's NOT fair but it's what we do." Most of us spend hours we don't have trying to justify why something IS fair, and we frequently run out of reasons, because the bottom line is that in fact it ISN'T! However, the next standard response is: "Who ever told you life was fair?" This, along with a rehash of the basic policies on which the procedure is based, will suffice, and the complaints will then diminish. The main positive aspect of this choice, rather than having rules that some people can break, is that the general policy of living by the family rules is upheld, and the message received is that cooperation and compliance with procedures is expected and appreciated. It also reinforces the message that each individual will be treated according to his or her needs, going back to the notion that trainees are NOT in fact equal, they are different personalities with different demands and different ways of interacting with the environment.

It is probably important to note that trainees frequently do not agree with certain procedures, and that it does no harm for management to acknowledge this disagreement or (heaven forbid) actually to sympathize with them that it really doesn't seem that fair. At this point, suffice it to say that *disagreement from the ranks neither mandates nor even implies a need for policy or procedural change*. Later we shall get to the issue of whose choice it is to follow a procedure and its consequences, and who therefore has the bottom line control.

## Job Descriptions

All family members have some basic developmental tasks to do. These will vary depending on age and stage (i.e., a young child's need to trust her environment, the adolescent's search for identity and independence, an adult's mid-life crisis, etc.). These need to be taken into account in the general understanding of job descriptions. They are not an excuse to abdicate family responsibilities.

Management teams that are satisfied with the balance of power, the division of responsibilities and their roles as partners are generally more confident in managing the company. If there are two original managers, the trainees require input from both. This does not mean equal roles, it simply means job sharing. Children benefit the most when their two original managers remain committed to their training and well-being, are accepting of their inexperience, and work together in the same general direction to ensure skill-building and increasing independence over the years. There is no question that life is less confusing and the training more consistent when these managers remain in the same company. This does not mean that single-manager, multi-branch companies, or merged corporations cannot work, or work reasonably well. The main problem is that when original companies split up, there is frequently a high level of acrimony over such management issues as who is in charge of what physical plant, how the finances will be handled, and who gets which trainees at which times. These management issues can be so intense that the trainees' issues often become low priority.

It would be foolish to say that management teams, even when totally committed to the family's best interests, always agree on management responsibilities and division of labour. They don't. It is tempting to say that perhaps they shouldn't. Life could get very stagnant. However, children or trainees do not have a place in determining how management should or should not cope with management level decisions about who-does-what. In fact, children's responses in such situations are wonderfully predictable — they will side with whoever puts the least pressure on THEM. Therefore, management needs to sort out the who-does-what-when-and-how behind the closed doors of a management meeting. The media would love to have us believe that public accountability overrides the rights of groups to hold closed meetings, and perhaps they are right in some circumstances. However, they are NOT right when it comes to families. There are strong reasons why management should meet out of the earshot of children. In single-child families, there is often a compelling feeling of needing to include the child to prevent him from feeling left out. Trust me, feeling left out is a lot more appropriate than feeling you have a role in determining management's responsibilities. If one manager or the other insists that children should be present at discussions about management personnel or duties, there is something wrong within the management team. If both parents insist on discussing management issues in front of the trainees, there is something wrong with the whole structure of the company. In either case, this needs to be worked on before policy, procedures or other issues can be dealt with.

This does not mean that there is *never* a place for a family meeting to discuss the implementation of new management job descriptions. It simply means that parents have to work it out first and only then put it to the trainees. For example, children might be told: "Dad and I have talked about who is going to drive you to hockey, and we have decided to take turns"; or "From now on, Mom will be responsible for deciding who does what chores, so it's no good coming to me for that"; or even "Your father and I have decided that we are not going to make any major decisions about you guys until we have had a chance to talk it over." This is especially important if there have been management differences of opinion over following through with the consequences of a child's choices, as in: "Mom and I have decided that when you choose to spend your whole allowance within an hour of getting it, we are not going to advance you ANY money at all until the next allowance day, so there's no use trying it on."

## Employment Equity?

Within families, rather than being primarily a gender-based issue, employment equity issues have more to do with perception of equal rights and privileges. The following are facts of life:

1.  Management and trainees do not have similar privileges, since they do not have the same job descriptions, experience, body of knowledge, obligations, accountability or responsibility.

2.  Trainees are not equal, either to management or to each other. They
    are different personalities who require different styles of management.
    Seniority is a fact of life. To treat trainees equally is to deny their dif-
    ferences.

Job descriptions are therefore different for each member of the company. There is generally no reason for them to be identical, even if trainees
are identical twins, since jobs in a Total Quality Management company are
geared to the strengths, skills and needs of each individual, with responsibilities for different jobs being handed over to the individual doing that
job, once that person is capable of assuming that responsibility. The job
may be supervised for a while, then delegated. Reinforcement generally
comes from receiving the approval of those who have trusted you with the
responsibility, and eventually from the inner satisfaction that arises from a
job well done. The message here isn't a new one. "If you give him a fish,
he eats for a day; if you teach him to fish, he eats for a lifetime."

On the journey from total dependence as a newborn, to total independence upon leaving home, children have to move from having us do things
for them, through being directed, through being coached, through being
prompted, to doing things all by themselves. Job descriptions must therefore take account of what the child's developmental level enables him to
do, and more importantly of what our needs are in continuing to do things
for him—sometimes WE need to give him that fish much more than he
needs to be given it. Management responsibilities for child-centred goals
will change and diminish with time, as children become more capable and
skilled at doing things for themselves.

## Rules of Thumb for Job Descriptions

The main rules of thumb about providing job descriptions to trainees are
fairly simple to state, even if not so easy to do.

1.  Ensure that the job description is written in terms of what the trainee
    IS expected to do, and not what is NOT expected. It is extremely
    difficult and frustrating for individuals to follow procedures if they
    consist of all the things that you must not do, i.e., "don't hit your sis-
    ter," "don't yell," "if you don't…you won't…," "you shouldn't…,"
    and so on. It would also be hard to remain content and motivated in

the workplace if you were given your whole year's salary at the outset and then had it clawed back piece by piece when you did not perform properly. Wording expectations positively and providing positive feedback for cooperation are two important factors in gaining compliance from trainees. This is outlined in detail later when we talk about Management Strategies.

2. Ensure that the job has been clearly explained by having the trainee put in her own words what it is she's expected to do. If it is simply parroted back to you, it may not have traveled through any active part of the brain.

3. Ensure that the job is within the capabilities of the trainee if you expect independent performance. If it is not, provide additional training, and help out until the skills are developed. Even small children can do jobs such as putting their empty juice box in the garbage. You may find out the limits of your child's capabilities only when they fail. Support them when this happens and allow them to learn from their mistakes.

4. *Expect* that the job will be done. Try not to forget to *acknowledge* that it has been done. ("It's about time!" doesn't cut it.)

5. Expect that the job will not be done as well as you would like it to be done. Do praise the effort.

6. Encourage children to use lists or notes or other visual reminders to help them remember what to do.

7. Model what you want them to do. Children, like adults, learn far more from watching the picture than by listening to the soundtrack. Talk to yourself as you do things (you are neither senile nor crazy). Children need to hear you solve problems and make mistakes *outside* of your head. This helps them sort out their own jobs.

8. If you find yourself saying, "I've told you again and again," stop talking. Chances are your trainee has stopped listening. Use more creative ways of reminding. A compost bucket in the middle of a bed speaks volumes. Collected belongings in a garbage bag in the basement teach a more memorable lesson than endless nagging. An empty plate at dinner may trigger the thought that the dog needs food.

9.  Make sure to delegate whenever you can. Many children who demand control over inappropriate decisions may not have many decisions over which they DO have control. It really doesn't matter if their socks don't match if they had control over choosing them.

10. Do not underestimate your child's ability to take responsibility, but do not *overestimate* it either. Try letting out the rope a little, but be certain to watch for dangerous-looking loops. You can always try a new way of doing things for a few days or weeks, and reevaluate its success.

## Performance Evaluations

As parents, we get very little feedback as to the quality of job we are doing. In fact, for the most part, we rely on our children's comments, behaviour and report cards for our evaluation. The comments primarily consist of "I hate you!" "You're SO mean!" "You're not my REAL dad!" "Everybody ELSE's parents let them!"—none of which is particularly satisfying. Most of us don't hear "You're just the greatest!" except for those memorable Mother's Day or Father's Day projects in the primary grades of school, or when our children want something. As to our children's behaviour, while this may be one of the more valid means of evaluation, we can be rather too vigilant, claiming credit for all the successes and blaming ourselves for all the failures or inadequacies. We sometimes forget that our children have hundreds of other influences shaping their performance in life, some quite significant, such as teachers, friends, extended family and the media. I have always felt that schools do not really understand the impact of report cards, particularly in the primary years, in that a failing grade for "Works well with others" or "Interacts well with peers" is frequently taken as a failing grade in parenting.

Sometimes in a therapy situation, we have the chance to take a look at general "performance evaluations" as a way to understand what is happening in the family, particularly with older teenagers who are struggling for change. These cannot be done successfully while the room is bouncing with emotion, and so the feelings usually need to be recognized, reflected, acknowledged and validated before working on the more objective assessment and goal-setting phase.

 *Nancy (aged 17) had been complaining of bad headaches that appeared to be associated with negative moods. She stated clearly*

*that finding ways of coping with the headaches was the only reason she had agreed to come. She had been thoroughly checked over by a neurologist who had cleared her of any physical problems and who had subsequently referred her for stress management. There were many complaints from her parents about the high levels of conflict within the family due to Nancy's bad temper, angry outbursts, open hostility and sometimes aggression toward her two younger brothers. In fact, it was very difficult for Nancy's parents, particularly Mom who was also very stressed by the home situation, to say anything positive at all about their first-born. For Nancy's part, there were grumbles about Mom being "too picky," Mom and Dad "never listening" and "always judging," along with the perennial "everything in the house is ALWAYS my fault" and "I'm NEVER allowed to do ANYthing."*

*As in many situations of family conflict, it is frequently quite difficult to settle down to initiating change in the face of high levels of negative emotion. So after some individual sessions with Nancy and a couple of management meetings with Mom and Dad where we gave plenty of air time to the negative feelings, Nancy was able to work on performance evaluations for both her parents as well as herself that could be kept fairly free of emotion.*

**Dad:**

| | |
|---|---|
| ***Areas of strength:*** | *considerate* |
| | *laid-back* |
| | *tolerant of mess* |
| | *follows through with what he says, predictable* |
| | *"Mr. Fix-It," in charge of maintenance at home* |
| ***Areas for improvement:*** | *needs to let others take more responsibility* |
| | *needs to let others express independent opinions* |
| | *needs to let people take care of their own lives* |

**Mom:**

*Areas of strength:*          cares about our education,
                                     safety and health
                              always knows when we are sick,
                                     takes care of us
                              very organized
                              does our taxes, is the family
                                     "accountant"
                              "manager" of the household,
                                     cooks and cleans


*Areas for improvement:*      needs to change from "lecturing"
                                     to "discussing"
                              needs to let people exercise their
                                     own judgment
                              needs to let people make their
                                     own decisions

**Self-evaluation:**

*Areas of strength:*          chooses friends from similar
                                     background
                              does well in school
                              chooses appropriate
                                     after-school activities
                              enthusiastic
                              likes to try new things


*Areas for improvement:*      needs to improve happiness level
                              needs to stop taking anger out on
                                     others in family
                              needs to allow people to
                                     show affection


With Nancy's permission, these evaluations were shared with Mom and Dad, and we were able to set some common goals for the family and to start to work towards these.

## What Gets in the Way?

Given that we have followed all of these guidelines, why is it that children still don't get the job done? Whether it's homework, walking the dog, or tidying up, there seems to be a need for constant reminders. There are an infinite number of issues that can get in the way—from lack of understanding to plain defiance and all stops in between. Passive aggression (i.e., doing nothing so that you irritate other people) is quite common in families, just as strikes are a tool used by employees to get management to give in under various circumstances. There is also the very real possibility that what is being asked is not reasonable. Parents with low self-esteem, or with unfinished issues from their own first families, will frequently assume the latter and will back off. It is important to have someone in your life who can provide an objective reality check. It is not the purpose of this book to cover all of these issues, and some suggested readings are listed at the back. The following are just a few examples from the family management model that can be considered if you are having trouble in the area of compliance.

It is hard to know what your job is if the guidelines keep changing, or if one manager tells you to do something and the other manager tells you that you don't have to do it. It is also very difficult to be a part-time employee in two different companies with two different jobs, especially when one of the managers keeps telling you how dumb the other company's rules are, even though you can't do anything about it.

Whenever anyone leaves the company or becomes temporarily or permanently incapacitated, or whenever anyone joins the company (manager or trainee), there will be a shift in job description for all other members of the company. Often, this shift is not obvious and/or is never discussed. Family meetings can be very useful to make sure that changes become an open agenda item and that everyone is aware of what everyone else's job is.

As trainees become more experienced and competent, they are able to take on more responsibility and to function more independently. Different requirements evolve as children develop. Therefore, job descriptions tend to change with time. Again, these shifts are often not obvious, since they tend to happen gradually. Reevaluation of job descriptions will happen without conscious effort most of the time. Sometimes it will be necessary to make the effort. This means that messages such as "but everyone else's parents let them…" or "no one else's family…" or "all my friends…" need to be considered every once in a while as a reality check. Remember, constructive suggestions can be considered and discounted just as well as they can be considered and incorporated.

The vast majority of children's behavioural difficulties seem to involve some problem with the youngster's understanding of or adherence to his job description.

> **It is virtually impossible to work on trainee job descriptions until policies are in place, management responsibilities are clear, general operating procedures are clarified, everyone understands what is expected of everyone else, these expectations are communicated clearly *and* compliance is warmly appreciated.**

It is therefore both necessary and important to take the time to go through and check out whether these issues have been explored and are in place. Otherwise, job descriptions are given in a bit of a vacuum and therefore may seem arbitrary, or imposed for the sake of imposing. If trainees are somewhat aware of the general direction of the company and can see the role they are playing, it is so much easier to understand why things have to be done and how their tasks are important in the bigger picture.

# 7

# Money Matters
# —to Pay or Not to Pay?

One of the most common questions asked by family managers concerns remuneration for trainees in the form of allowances or payment for jobs done. A lot of work is often needed within a family in order to sort out the complexities behind a deceptively simple question like "How much allowance is reasonable for a 10-year-old?" or "Do you think children should get allowances?"

Since there is no simple right or wrong answer to these questions, and since conflict over finances rates as one of the top two Major Incident Triggers in relationships, let us use the Family Management Model to try to provide a framework for resolving such issues. This requires us to determine who the players are (structure), what the general philosophies are (policies) and what the expectations are (procedures). Then we can see whether our procedures are in fact in line with our policies and in particular with the value systems that we are trying to model for our children. The following examples illustrate various different approaches and their potential consequences.

## Remuneration Policy:  The Jones Family

**Structure:**          *Intact family; permanent trainees.*

*Policy:*              *In our family, parents are the providers for the children.*

*Procedures:*          *Whenever the children need something, they ask Mom*
                       *or Dad to buy it for them, or ask for the money to get it*
                       *for themselves.*

*Conflicts:*           *As they are getting older, Mom and Dad increasingly do*
                       *not approve of what the children want to buy or how*
                       *often they are asking for money.*

*Messages:*            *"My parents are always there to provide for me."*
                       *"When I want something, I ask my parents."*
                       *"When I want something, someone will provide it*
                       *    for me."*
                       *"I am not responsible for earning what I need."*
                       *"My parents have control over what I have or*
                       *    don't have."*
                       *"The kids are constantly demanding."*
                       *"The kids expect me to pay all the time; they don't*
                       *    know when enough is enough."*

The dilemma here arises largely from the inner guilt parents feel if they see themselves as NOT being there to provide for their children. Hence, this approach to remuneration is frequently used beyond the time when it might be appropriate (i.e., when children are far too young to manage money), and well into the resentment phase with its overwhelming feeling of being used. There is a need to balance the parent-as-provider aspect of management with the need to train the children to budget and to make decisions about spending, about their needs and about their capabilities to provide for their own needs.

## Remuneration Policy: The Lalonde Family

*Structure:*           *Blended family; part-time trainees from both original*
                       *companies.*

*Policy:*              *In our family, money does not grow on trees; you have*
                       *to earn whatever you need.*

*Procedures:*      *Children are not given an allowance —partly because of general policy, partly because there are issues of child support that cause problems. Each household chore is assigned a set amount of money (e.g., 50 cents for doing dishes, $2 for cleaning room, $2 for vacuuming, etc.) and whoever does the chore gets paid for it.*

*Conflicts:*      *There is constant bickering over who does what. Parents try to enforce chores. One child does not care about the money so never does anything. Another child does chores only when she needs the money. A third child expects money even if the chores are not done completely or to Mom's or Dad's satisfaction. Another problem is that the parents frequently forget who did what and there are arguments over who is owed what and who has or hasn't been paid.*

*Messages:*      *"If I work at this particular job, I know how much I will be paid."*
*"If I want more money, I can do more work to get it."*
*"If I don't need money, I don't have to do anything around the house."*
*"If I don't get paid, I don't have to do it."*
*"Adults don't live up to their part of the deal."*
*"Household chores are jobs that you do if you need money."*
*"If none of the kids needs money, Mom or Dad will do all the chores."*
*"I only have to help out around the house if I need something."*

This situation poses its own dilemmas. Most families generally want to teach children that you have to work for what you want in life, and that work sometimes brings its own rewards. However, in this case, there is an overriding message that the reason we do things to help out at home is simply so that we can be paid for it. The values that most parents want to teach usually also include the one about "In this family, we all get to help each other," or perhaps "In this family, we all have family work to do." Thus, there may be competing values, and management may have to take a look at resolving some of the conflicting messages, perhaps by teaching children that life frequently involves competing value systems, and helping them to deal with the contradictions. There are, however, some good arguments to be made for NOT tying regular, help-us-all-out chores to remuneration of any kind when the we-all-help-out value is an important message within the family.

## Remuneration Policy: The Johanssen Family

*Structure:*      *Two single-parent households; trainees ship back and forth.*

*Policy:*      *__At Dad's__, we believe that parents should provide for their children (as in Jones Family above).*
*__At Mom's__, money does not grow on trees; you have to earn what you need (as in Lalonde Family above).*

*Procedures:*      *__At Dad's__, each child is given a generous allowance of "mad money" with which to buy whatever they want, and Dad decides what he will or won't buy the children in addition to this (usually determined by bickering with Mom about what it is or is not his duty to provide as per the separation agreement). There are no chores because it's a weekend and children need their fun time. Besides, Dad has a cleaning lady.*
*__At Mom's__, the children are assigned chores appropriate to their age and are expected to do them. Mom uses chore time as a time to spend chatting to the children as they work, while she gets on with some jobs of her own. Should they wish to earn extra money or privileges for something specific, there are additional, optional "jobs" that can be done and "banked" for that particular purpose.*

*Conflicts:*      *The children think Mom should do things the way Dad does them, and this sets off some heated discussions between Mom and Dad, with each one telling the other one how they should run their company and treat their trainees. The children are caught between having what-*

*ever they want with Dad and alienating Mom in the process. They are acting out in both places.*

*Messages:*
> *"Dad is a great guy."*
> *"Mom is mean; she never gives us anything."*
> *"Mom is always controlling what I spend!"*
> *"When I have money, I can buy whatever I want with it."*
> *"I always have to do work at Mom's; we never have to do ANYthing at Dad's!"*
> *"Chores are something that someone ELSE should be doing."*
> *"I get to spend time with my Mom when I'm doing my chores."*
> *"I have a way of getting special things if I really want them."*
> *"Grown-ups have quite different ideas about money!"*
> *"Dad's just trying to buy us; I wish he'd DO something with us instead."*

A lot of major and hidden dilemmas here—in a very complicated situation. Competing messages between parents; yet a sense of predictability for the children, either in a self-indulgent way, or in a rather resigned way. It can be hoped that both parents and children will eventually understand the difference between controlling and guiding, and between generosity and irresponsibility, and that trainees will at some point appreciate the short-term pain suffered in pursuit of the long-term gain. It is difficult for parents in this situation to reach a compromise that will enable the children to sort out the contradictions. However, each parent is consistent in their *own* policy, and children can learn to live with this. It will not resolve the intrinsic value differences between the managers which probably contributed in large part to the dissolution of the original company.

## Remuneration Policy: The Brown Family

*Structure:*      *Intact family; permanent trainees*

*Policy:*          *In this family, we believe that individuals need to be responsible about money.*

*Procedures:*     The children receive a weekly allowance based on what
                  they generally like to buy (i.e., some junk food, rent a
                  video, hockey cards, etc.), **instead** of parents buying
                  these things for them. Parents then double this amount
                  to constitute the full weekly allowance, but insist that
                  half the money be put aside to save for a larger item, a
                  special trip, or long-term wants  Additional money can
                  be earned from part-time jobs, such as babysitting,
                  mowing neighbours' lawns, paper routes, delivering fly-
                  ers for the church, and so on. As they get older, children
                  are given a clothing allowance to cover all except large
                  ticket necessities, again instead of, not in addition to,
                  parents buying clothing. Money is neither lent to nor
                  borrowed from the children. If the allowance is insuffi-
                  cient to meet a particular need, the need has to be put
                  on hold. In a real emergency, or unforeseen circum-
                  stance, parents will discuss helping out.

*Conflicts:*      The children are starting to use their money for things
                  parents do not condone (i.e., cigarettes, designer cloth-
                  ing, presents for friends, etc.).

*Messages:*       "It's my money, I can do what I like with it."
                  "If I need something, I have to save up for it."
                  "Saving up takes time and effort, but it's worth it."
                  "My parents trust me."
                  "When the money is spent, there is no more."
                  "Money doesn't grow on trees."
                  "I believe that I'm responsible with my money."
                  "My parents take my money issues seriously and
                       treat me like a grown-up."

The main dilemma here arises when our children start to spend money
we are providing to them on habits or items of which we simply cannot
approve. It could be drugs, not just cigarettes, they are buying. This is the
time when we might want to consider withdrawing our financial support.
Given that they have already learned that they can earn money by working
for it, they will always have a source of money, but this is part of letting
go, when as parents we have to realize that we cannot always control every

aspect of what our children do. We do not, however, have to pay for it. We can deal with issues around smoking, drugs and other lifestyle "habits" in other ways than making it an issue of who pays. We can institute a whole new bag of policies and procedures, in fact. We tend to find out that the policy "we don't do things because we can't afford to" doesn't hold up in a strong wind once our children have their own money. We need to develop different policies that allow us to address major issues from a completely different angle.

# 8

# Labour Relations

One of the main purposes of the family company is to train the children in management techniques and strategies so that they can become competent managers themselves. This is a lengthy process, usually lasting up to 18 or more years, during which children gradually take on increasing responsibilities for decision making. At the same time, parents gradually have to let go of these responsibilities. The balance between these two processes is delicate and sometimes even fragile, as mistakes are made on both sides. Children are initially not very good at making the choices that are involved in good decision making. They rarely have access to the same information or experiences that adults do, even if they think they do. One of the problems of modern families, as explained so articulately by Mary Pipher in her book *The Shelter of Each Other*, is that children in fact have access not only to vast amounts of information that we adults did not have access to at their age, but also that we STILL as adults do not have access to this information. There is a great danger, however, in assuming that access to information alone makes us good decision makers. The benefits of years of experience and exposure to the social world around us can never be underestimated.

Children are NOT, as many people presume, simply little adults. They think DIFFERENTLY and base their decisions on a whole different type of logic than adults do. They are very inexperienced in knowing how to deal with the consequences of their decisions and are not always even equipped to do so. They cannot function without the guidance and discipline provided by parents, even if they think they can.

The purpose of this chapter is not to provide a recipe for how to deal with specific issues, or even to go into great detail about what specific techniques to use for consequences, rewards and "punishments" in given situations. There are plenty of superb books already available that deal with problem solving. Here, we will examine some of the issues that are basic to negotiating with children, giving choices where choices are appropriate, with a view to enabling managers to understand why orders may not be followed nor advice taken. We'll also provide some guidance for handing over decision making to the troops.

The journey of learning for the trainees is a continuous progression from total dependence as a newborn to the total independence that signals the end of adolescence. As we have discussed elsewhere, this means that managers have to move from doing everything for the trainee to enabling the trainee to do everything for herself. This is accomplished best by understanding decision making and choices, and making the major transition from commanding to advising.

## General Principles of Labour Relations and Negotiations in Families

In order to benefit from each other's strengths and skills, good communication within the company is critical. Both management and trainees need processes by which they can communicate information, feelings, opinions, concerns, advice, policy decisions, procedural matters, pats on the back, and so forth. Here are some of the *general principles*:

Some decisions are *absolute*—usually with respect to safety and health—and thus are non-negotiable.

If the non-negotiable is negotiated, it is obviously *not* non-negotiable. In non-negotiable situations, there are no choices.

In non-negotiable situations, management gives orders. Orders may be followed by the imposition of consequences.

If orders are disguised as advice, questions, suggestions, requests or opinions, trainees may find it hard to tell the difference.

Natural consequences are the most effective, followed by logical consequences, followed by arbitrary consequences.

Maturity means accepting the consequences of your choices.

While there are times when promises cannot be kept and times when it is not appropriate for promises to be kept, damaged trust takes time to heal.

In a Managed Family environment, management listens actively to trainee suggestions, ideas and opinions, acknowledges the contributions, and makes decisions regarding their viability.

In a Managed Family, trainees feel free to express opinions without expecting management to act on them.

In a Managed Family, trainees know that management has a long-term commitment to making the family work.

Management will attempt to help trainees make informed choices, and will permit them to learn from the inevitable mistakes that will be made along the way.

## Choices

**Major Assumption: If an issue is non-negotiable, there is no choice.**

In many circumstances, however democratic your philosophy, your child in fact does not have a choice. For most families, the following are non-negotiable: running across the road in front of a speeding truck; eating something that is hazardous to health; taking medication for a life-threatening disorder; seatbelts; and so on. Each family has its own set of non-negotiables; there is no universal set that is "right." Most families take non-negotiables as "givens," and little or no time is wasted negotiating them. Non-negotiables may change from time to time because of circumstances— and following a management decision. For example, what a child wears may be largely negotiable unless it is for a special occasion, such as a wedding. Such changes may be confusing and precipitate conflict. If a non-negotiable continually changes, it will be perceived as negotiable. Trainees tend to think that it is unfair that management has sole rights to change a negotiable issue into a non-negotiable one and vice versa. It may be unfair, but that's life.

### If a child attempts to negotiate the non-negotiable, he thinks it's negotiable.

This is an important issue to recognize, because vast quantities of time and energy can be wasted over long periods of time stuck in negotiations about something that is not negotiable. If an issue is non-negotiable, even discussing whether it should or should not be negotiable is off-limits. A request by a trainee for management to reconsider a non-negotiable issue may be made in an appropriate tone of voice at an appropriate time, along with constructive suggestions and appropriate support for a potential change. Management may then choose whether or not to consider such a motion. In order to avoid conflict, power struggles and industrial sabotage, it is preferable for management to discuss the issue prior to bringing a decision back to the trainees.

### Many issues have non-negotiable and negotiable components.

Bedtime routines are typical situations that have both components. The fact that your child needs to go to sleep at night is generally not negotiable, even in the most *laissez-faire* of families. Where and when he is expected to be in bed, with teeth cleaned and lights out, may also generally be non-negotiable issues as far as parents are concerned, although many children seem to feel that they have a vote in these areas. Some other aspects of bedtime routines may or may not be negotiable, depending on family priorities, for example, a back rub, story, second glass of water, extra hug and kiss, etc. Decide on which aspects are non-negotiable and make them direct and clear—then negotiate the others.

### Some situations are negotiable until a decision is made.

In families where there is adequate communication and a general belief in cooperation and consensus, there may be discussion prior to a procedure being put into place. Once the discussion has taken its course and each individual's opinions have been considered, management has the job of deciding when an issue or procedure becomes non-negotiable.

**Management needs to agree on what is non-negotiable.**

Because of the impact and power of non-negotiable issues in families, it is extraordinarily difficult for trainees if management continually contradicts itself as to what the rules are. Even though management may not agree on negotiable issues, and may have different guidelines for those, it is important to work for agreement on the non-negotiables, even if the list has to be shortened. This is especially true for reconstituted families, since both managers, regardless of original company, need to uphold the non-negotiables.

**If there is no choice, do not give one.**

If a situation is not negotiable and there is no choice, it is important not to imply that there is a choice. "Would you like to come to Grandma's with us on Sunday?" "Do you mind switching off the TV and coming to supper?" "Could you put your things away now and get ready for bed?" are all examples of questions that can be answered with the word "no." Non-negotiable situations require direct instruction or orders.

**Free choices set everyone up.**

A free choice (for example: "What would you like for breakfast?") implies a free range of responses (for example: "coke and a chocolate chip cookie" or "nothing"). Do not give a free choice unless you are prepared to live with a free range of responses or with your child's righteous indignation when you refuse to honour the choice. The message frequently is: "Sorry, you guessed wrong; guess again!"

**Try to give a selection of choices, even if it's "take it or leave it!"**

Almost all situations provide the opportunity for choice of some kind, unless the issue is non-negotiable. Give your child a selection of choices from which to pick—and stick with the pick! The following are a small sample of possible choices: "Would you like cheese or carrot sticks for your snack?" "Would you like to come home at 8:30 or 9:00?" "Would you like me to pick you up at 11:30 or would you prefer not to go?" "Would you like to speak to me in a pleasant voice so that I can hear you, or would you prefer to go to your room?" "Would you like to go to your room right now or would you prefer to lose TV for the rest of the day?" "The door will stay open if you choose to stay in bed after I have said goodnight, or the door will be shut if you decide to get up again."

**Choices enable your child to take responsibility and to be accountable.**

Recognize that giving choices provides your child with some measure of control within your general management strategy; it does not hand over the reins. This permits total quality management in that your child can take over the choices in those areas where he has the competence and skills within the general parameters of your family management policies and practices. It means that your child is, in fact, in charge of his own consequences, and you are no longer the "bad cop." When your child gets mad because he has chosen to miss a favourite TV show by choosing not to complete homework or a chore, he is in fact mad at himself and not at anyone else. This interesting fact may need to be pointed out on occasion.

**Start using the word "choice" instead of "rule."**

This small wording change is significant and powerful. It emphasizes the shift of responsibility, makes life much more pleasant for management, and sets up a situation where natural or logical consequences can be implemented. It is important to start using it in your head and rehearsing how it sounds so that you are more likely to use it in real-life situations.

**Positive choices are more effective than negative ones.**

Try to phrase choices as POSITIVELY as possible. This makes for a much more pleasant situation for both parties than trying to decide between a rock and a hard place. "When you have..., then you may..." is a good phrase to start with, since this leads to the inevitable "...and if you haven't, then you may not..." which can, for the most part, remain unspoken unless necessary. Try not to offer a choice between punishments, although this remains an option. Although you are offering a choice when you say "Jason, stop bugging Jennifer or you will be sent to your room," you are still ordering and punishing. It will probably be more effective to say "Jason, you have a choice. You can play nicely with Jennifer, or you can go and play by yourself in your room. It's up to you."

### Label the choices clearly.

If either you or your child are having difficulty understanding the choices, deliberately use the word "choice" in your conversation, finishing up with "It's up to you." For example: "Melissa, you have a choice. You can either switch off the TV right away and come to supper, or I can switch it off for you. Which would you prefer? It's up to you."

### Follow through.

Unless absolutely impossible because of drastically changed circumstances, it is CRITICAL to follow through with the promise you have made to your child. Remember that the consequence you are providing is your child's own choice. You are NOT the bad guy! You do not therefore have to back down or apologize, or feel badly for following through. Your child may have to be mad at himself, not at you. The fact that you have given a choice at all probably limits the number of times the child is grounded for life, but if he chose being grounded for life rather than complying with a company by-law, hey, that's his decision!

### Offer only those choices you can live with.

This is a very important aspect of this whole strategy. You do not have to entertain any alternative choices and consequences put forward by your child, although of course you may if you wish, provided they are feasible and you can live with them. Don't split hairs. If your child's "new" choice is, in fact, one of yours slightly reworded, let the child's choice stand—it is a good bargaining strategy and makes the child feel effective. As mentioned earlier, giving a selection of choices gives your trainee some control. This is especially important for those children who are born strong-willed. However, if you get stuck with a choice you wish you had never given, or that you are totally unwilling to support, you have set both of you up for a high-conflict situation. Your child will not trust the system, and the struggle for supremacy will continue.

It is generally not appropriate for trainees to give management choices, unless the trainees are extremely sophisticated and diplomatic. This is one of the many unfair labour practices that are alive and well.

### Threats can easily be reframed as choices.

This makes them easier to swallow—and to enforce. "If you don't get on with your homework, you won't watch TV" becomes "If you choose to do your homework, you'll also be choosing to watch TV later." Parents are far more likely to follow through with promises than with threats.

### Consider trainees' ideas; they are often creative and useful.

Trainees occasionally have good ideas that are useful to the running of the family company. Management can take each and every idea, however loony, as a possible option (acknowledgment does not signify assent) and get back to the trainees once they have had a chance to debate, consider and make a decision.

### Life is indeed not fair.

Seniority and competence are important elements involved in the selection of choices offered to trainees. Therefore, not all trainees are given identical choices. Even the most junior trainee is, however, capable of making a simple choice.

### Watch the picture.

Words alone do not count, and if a trainee shows by her behaviour that she clearly is not yet capable of making a particular type of choice, you may have to back down on the decision to give her that level of choice. It is usually possible to simplify the choice being offered. For example, if an older adolescent chooses an hour at which to be home and sticks to that choice, your concerns regarding trust and safety are in large part met. However, if he chooses not to be home at that time, this level of autonomy may well be beyond his capabilities, and he may have to choose between being home at a given time or not having the option of taking your car. Younger children may choose to stay up later than usual, but be unable to control their emotions because of tiredness, in which case they may lose the choice. Even though the child TELLS you that he is not tired, the picture shows differently.

### Trainees sometimes live life by default.
### Help them recognize choices.

Older teens tend to make their own choices and inform you about them if you are lucky. It may be necessary for you to remind them on occasion that they are indeed making a choice; they do not always realize it and feel that they are controlled by others or live life by default. "Well, it seems to me that you had a choice. You decided not to let me know that you'd be home for supper, so I didn't get any food ready."

### But what about me?

Always remember that you, also, have choices. You can choose what you do with your own time, effort, material goods, services and money. There are no rules anywhere that mandate justifying any of these. It is not written anywhere in the Parent's Manual that you HAVE TO drive your child anywhere, HAVE TO pay for leisure choices that you do not approve of, HAVE TO support financially any unacceptable lifestyle choices, HAVE TO do laundry, HAVE TO lend the car, HAVE TO explain why not, and so on *ad nauseam*.

## Non-Negotiables—or "Yes, It's an Order!"

**Major Assumption:  When an issue is non-negotiable, it is appropriate for management to give trainees orders.**

Most parents, especially those who like to see themselves as warm and supportive, prefer to ask than to tell. However, when an issue is non-negotiable and there are no choices, and when asking does not produce the desired response, it is completely appropriate, often necessary, for parents to give their children orders or commands. This clarifies for children where the limits are and provides a safe boundary within which they can relax and develop.

### Orders are not negotiable.

"Turn off the TV now and get on with your homework." This gives an "...or else" air to them. They are definite and non-negotiable.

### Orders may be worded in many different ways.

Orders can be softened by saying "I would appreciate it if you would..."

or "please...," as in: "Please put your toys away and get your coat on" or "I would appreciate it if you would pick up your dirty laundry." It is quite important to establish this when the child is very young; it teaches by example and provides the basis for mutual respect. There are many times, however, when you have to drop the frills and be very direct.

**Orders work better when they are worded in terms of what IS required, rather than what is not.**

For example, "Please pick up your boots from the front hall and put them in the closet," sounds and works better than "Please don't leave your boots in the front hall." This gives children a non-judgmental job description, rather than a comment on the likelihood of them doing something wrong. It also enables positive reinforcement for a job properly done.

**Orders normally require a consequence.**

Because of the "or else" flavour to an order, a consequence is required. When an order is worded negatively, the consequence is almost always negative. When an order is worded positively, the consequence can be positive. Believe it or not, children will work for parental approval, even after puberty. It should not be necessary, and is definitely not advisable, to offer children all kinds of rewards for complying with everyday expectations. "There's a good boy!" "Thanks a lot!" "That was really helpful, thanks," are all examples of positive consequences for compliance. "It's about time!" is not. When trying to establish a new behaviour by changing an old one, it is especially important to reinforce the new behaviour as often as possible. Therefore, it is virtually impossible to reinforce positively an order such as "don't spit at your brother!" since even the most obnoxious child would spend quite a lot of time *not* doing this.

**Orders are useless if the consequences cannot be enforced.**

This does not mean that you have to be physically present to enforce consequences immediately. Trust, guilt and mutual respect can all work to have many children police themselves. However, the general rule of thumb is: only have rules that you are *willing* to enforce when necessary, and only have consequences that you are *able* to enforce.

**Orders phrased as questions frequently do not work.
Rephrase if necessary.**

While phrasing orders as questions is a gentler approach and can work sometimes with some children, when a child is asked a question, there is usually a range of choices for an answer. For example: "Would you like to come and have supper now?" "Would you like to come to the cottage on the weekend?" "Isn't it time to do your homework?" could each be answered "yes" or "no." If you already know the required answer, do not let your child feel that he or she has a choice when in fact there is none. A simple rephrasing will do: "It's time for supper, please come now," "We're all going to the cottage on the weekend," "It's time for homework," and so on.

**Orders are used more with younger children,
less as children get older.**

Children require and benefit from a clear job description. Thus, in the early trainee stages, there may well be a large number of orders. As children get older, the number of orders and consequences become less, as they take over more of the responsibility for their own behaviour. Be prepared to review your orders at various stages in your child's development.

**When policies are clearly understood, descriptive statements may
suffice, but be prepared to follow up with a direct order if necessary.**

For those of us who are lucky to have reasonably compliant children, and in families where there are clear policies in effect, it may sometimes be workable simply to describe what you see without adding an order, a suggestion or advice. "Your boots are in the middle of the front hall instead of in the closet" (policy: "We keep shared family space tidy at all times"; or "We are each responsible for our own things," etc.). "You left your dirty dish on the table" (policy: "We all do chores around here"; or "We are each responsible for our own things"; or "There are no servants in this house," etc.). "It's homework time" (policy: "Education takes priority in this house"; or "We all have things we must do, whether we want to or not," etc.). In the absence of an open, understood policy, and/or if the response from your child to "Your dirty clothes are all over the bathroom" is "SO?" you will need to add the order: "Please put them in the laundry basket."

**Requests can frequently be orders in a more pleasant disguise.**

"Would you please take out the garbage on your way out to the car?" may be a person-to-person request, just as you might ask a roommate to help out, or it may be an "or else." You need to be very clear in your own mind which one you mean. You may start off with a request, but end up with an order, depending on the response to the request.

**Non-compliance with requests may have different consequences than with orders.**

Thinking of your child as a roommate, rather than as a child, will help provide alternative perspectives as to what you might do when a request is not carried out. Failure to respond to "I wonder if you might pick up some milk for me on your way home," when addressed to a roommate, might well result in disappointment, lack of respect, reluctance to return a favour, and so forth, but is unlikely to result in the roommate being grounded or TV privileges being removed.

**Repeated and frequent non-compliance with requests means a change of tactic.**

A situation where there is continued non-compliance with requests usually suggests that the individual making the requests is becoming a doormat, or at least is not effective. This may be because the request is not direct enough, and your child may not realize that you are serious. Therefore a change of tactic is advisable. Decide whether you are in fact ordering or whether you are giving advice, less likely, but possible.

**When you realize that a request is no longer a request, you may need to share this insight.**

Children often do not realize that what has been a mild suggestion has changed into a order. Therefore, a verbal signal will help. "I'm no longer asking you, I'm telling you" is pretty direct.

**Repeated non-compliance with orders means you have a problem!**

Repeated non-compliance, even in the face of a directly worded order with a positive consequence for compliance, usually signals a need for a review of management strategy. There may need to be a new policy or procedure put in place, following a thorough review of the situation, including a meeting with the errant trainee(s) at which opinions can be expressed without any immediate, knee-jerk responses on either side (i.e., strike or lock-out, see page 113). Sometimes, the implementation of a Complaints Time can deal with negative feelings and encourage compliance with a procedure that is seen as "unfair" or "stupid." Sometimes, a specific procedure has become outmoded because the trainee has acquired new skills. It is a strong, responsive management team that can decide on a change of approach. However, it is important to get the message across to the trainees that any policy or procedural change is a management decision. Thank them for their input, and tell them you'll be trying it for a week to see how things go.

**Suggestions are often confused with orders or advice.**

This is especially true when they begin "I think you should..." or "Why don't you...". Sometimes when we say "I think you should wear mitts, it's cold outside," or "Why don't you phone her and ask," it sounds to some people like an order when in fact it may be intended as a suggestion. This is especially true if the suggestion is made by someone whose personality is quite powerful or overwhelming. It may be necessary for the recipient of this type of suggestion to clarify whether or not it is an order. "Mom, do you mean I HAVE to, or is it just that you think it would be a good idea?" This is the point at which to clarify whether the situation is non-negotiable or negotiable.

# Negotiables—Or Advice, Suggestions and Opinions

**Major Assumption: When a situation is negotiable, it is appropriate to offer opinions or advice, to ask whether someone would like to do something, or to make suggestion.**

It is definitely a significant parental responsibility to provide children with advice and suggestions, especially during the initial stages of the acquisition of a new skill or freedom. It is also one of the hardest habits to break, even when our children are running their own companies!

In situations where there is some room to manoeuvre, in the initial stages of the formulation of a new procedure or a change to an old one, and in fact in the large majority of interactions with children (especially adolescents) and others, the following may be helpful.

**Advice is advice. Suggestions are suggestions.
They may be taken or left.**

This means that you CANNOT follow up advice or a suggestion with a consequence! The consequence of not taking good advice is the other person's loss. Period. "It's cold outside, you might want to wear boots" is advice to a roommate. "It's cold outside, you *must* wear your boots" has the "or else" quality of an order, and therefore requires a consequence. You need to switch to an order if you suddenly realize you mean "do it."

**It is very hard to accept the change from orders to advice.**

This applies to both ends of the equation. It is hard for children who are accustomed to receiving orders to recognize that "I think you should..." now means that "I am giving you my opinion, take it or leave it, for what it's worth." They therefore tend to rebel, to become defensive, to become unnecessarily angry, or to say they don't care. They may also go along with it, resenting the perceived control when in fact parents did not intend to control. On the other hand, it is also extremely hard for parents to remember that they are switching from ordering to advising.

**The change from orders to advice comes primarily when there are
no longer consequences that can be upheld.**

Once parents realize, sometimes the hard way, that their older teenage children will no longer stay grounded and that they have no other consequences that they are able or willing to uphold, there may be little option other than to switch to advice and to allow natural consequences to take effect. While this is often extraordinarily hard to do, because of the safety and health factors that are frequently involved, there may seem to be no other choice.

**"If I were you ..."**

Communications that start with "If I were you..." signal advice or opinions, not orders. They may also signal a friendly warning of an imminent switch to orders: "If I were you, I would get my homework done before the TV gets turned off for the next week!"

**People own their own opinions.**

Whether we happen to agree with them or not, others' opinions are not wrong, only different, whether they happen to be management or trainees. This does not mean that a major shift in opinion never happens; of course it does, especially over time and with experience.  It is always helpful for a child to have his opinion acknowledged (i.e., "I realize that you feel you will be perfectly okay here on your own for the weekend") and considered (i.e., "Dad and I will talk it over and get back to you"). It is also pretty natural to try to change someone else's opinion when they disagree with us (i.e., "But surely you know that smoking is really bad for you"). There comes a point at which to acknowledge that we are not going to change the other's mind, and to try to do so is a colossal waste of time, however "dumb" their opinion may be! If you don't *have* to be right, there will be very little conflict.

**Differences of opinion do not necessarily lead to policy change.**

There are countless times in the life of a family company that dissenting opinions will be expressed; this is normal, natural and necessary. If, however, parents decide that a child's dissenting opinion means that policies or procedures must be changed in the absence of strong supporting information and simply in order to keep the child happy, the family management structure falls apart. In fact, it is far too powerful a situation for a child to realize that the fact that he does not agree with his parents is sufficient to cause the company to falter. Whether your child likes it or not, the garbage has to be taken out, the dog needs to be fed, education is important, and homework must be completed. She can be given endless sympathy for how awful or unfair she feels it is, but the job must still be done.

**Advice and opinions can become nagging if they are not acknowledged.**

If an individual feels that his advice or opinion has not been heard, he tends to repeat it many times over, sometimes in the same way, sometimes in different ways. When we do not happen to agree with the opinion or plan to take the advice, we tend to find it very hard to acknowledge that individual's viewpoint. However, this is a very effective way to bring a halt to repetitive conflicts or nagging. Simply paraphrasing what the person has said means that you have heard, not necessarily that you agree. "So I hear you saying that you don't think it's fair to make you do chores"; "So what you and Dad are saying is that you don't like me smoking"; "What you seem to be saying is that you think I shouldn't go out with her any more"; "I hear you—you think it's stupid."

## Important Issues In Communication

**Don't ever be afraid to clarify or label The negotiables and the non-negotiables.**

If either party—sender or receiver—is uncertain whether or not a given circumstance or issue is negotiable, it is very important for both parties to clarify the situation. Even individual communications can be labeled: "Is that an order or advice?" "This is a piece of advice," "If I were you...," "This is not negotiable," "You have a choice...," "In my opinion...," and so on. It is far better to ask or label than it is to assume!

**IF you decide to do something yourself when a request or order is not successful, that is your choice and your problem.**

If you get fed up with asking people to do what you want them to do and end up doing whatever it is yourself because it is easier, that is clearly something that you CHOOSE to do—no one is making you. Keep in mind what message this gives to others, and if you don't mind the particular message (i.e., "I don't have to do it, Mom will do it for me eventually"; "Dad is a pushover"; "Mom does everything for everyone, it's her job"), there's no reason to change. ***Don't complain. It was your choice.***

## Complaints Time

**Major Assumption: Children need a time to complain and to air their negative feelings in a setting where parents do not feel the need to fix everything.**

In many family companies, much agony is expended by both management and trainees over various issues that produce negative feelings. Life is not fair, chores are a burden, other siblings were sent into the world just to irritate, other children's families allow them to do anything they wish...the list is endless. Some children reach the point of apparent depression because their time with parents is spent in a litany of negative feelings.

The establishment of a set "Complaints Time" can serve two major purposes:

(a) it gives children a time when they know they will be listened to and when their feelings will be acknowledged; and
(b) it enables parents to stall complaints at other, less convenient times (for example, when the school bus is waiting at the curb, when you are off to work, ten minutes after "lights out," and so on) without feeling that you are shutting your child down.

The general policies being served by Complaints Time are:

• Children are entitled to hold and express opinions in this family.

• Parents listen to their children in this family.

• In this family, parents do not have to fix everything that bothers the children.

## Procedures For Complaints Time

1. Set aside a given period of time each day per child—for example, 10 to 15 minutes—preferably ending just before a favourite TV show or activity. Do not make it longer.

2. Set a TIMER to signal the end of the allotted time, or finish before that if your child runs out of complaints.

3. Call it "Complaints Time," not "Special Time" or "Tammy's Time." Make the intention clear and direct.

4. Remember that it is your child's complaints time, NOT yours.

5. LISTEN ACTIVELY, reflect or paraphrase. For example, when your child says: "It's not fair. Kristie is ALWAYS in my room, touching my stuff and ruining everything! She's a pain, and you are ALWAYS taking her side," you can say: "So you're saying that Kristie is always in your face and that you feel we're on her side." Try to rephrase negative comments if possible, so you are not later quoted out of context ("Mom says you're always in my face!"). If you are REALLY good at this, you may be able to be positively constructive: "So you are saying that you'd like our support in helping Kristie respect your privacy"—but this is not always possible in the heat of the moment!

6. LABEL and ACKNOWLEDGE feelings whenever possible, however much you may not understand or agree with them. "You are pretty angry at Kristie, I guess." "You seem very cross that Madame kept you in at recess." "You seem quite upset that Jeff was angry with you for taking his toys away." If in doubt, check it out. "How do you feel about that?" Whatever you do, DO NOT JUDGE feelings and DO NOT TELL her that she should not feel like that, even if you are trying to make her feel better.

7. Regardless of how much you want to, DO NOT FIX, RESOLVE, EDITORIALIZE, JUDGE or BLAME. Do not order, advise or suggest, and do not give your opinion, even if it is requested. Remind her that this is her time to talk, and that you need time to think it all over.

8. When the timer goes off, ask her if there are any more complaints for today. If there is just one more small one, allow it. If there is a whole list, tell her to jot down a few key words on an "agenda" for tomorrow. In this way, she will learn to get to the important stuff first. Anything that is not jotted down or is forgotten was not that important.

9. Thank her for sharing all this with you. Ask what, if anything, she would like you to do. Unless it is immediately life-threatening, tell her you will take it under advisement and get back to her.

10. Respect her wish that you do nothing—unless you, as management, consider the situation threatening, unsafe or abusive.

11. If there are ANY complaints in between sessions, ask her to add them

to the agenda which can be placed on the fridge, bulletin board, wherever. "That sounds like a good item for the Complaints Time agenda. Why don't you jot it down?" Again, if she cannot be bothered or forgets, it wasn't important.

12. Accept written complaints at any time for consideration at the next scheduled time.

13. Offer Complaints Time every day until she has not required it for three days in a row. Then tell her you will reinstitute it on request.

14. If there are two managers, take turns, even if your child initially balks at this. An imbalance will develop if only one of you hears all the complaints and shares all the negative feelings. Do not be surprised if you each hear a different range of complaints, with little or no overlap!

15. After a while, you may notice the same complaints recurring. If so, you may need to acknowledge more clearly that you have heard by paraphrasing more accurately. You may need to take some action. You may need to tell her that this is old news, think of something new.

16. Be careful of a situation where your child needs to complain in order to get you to herself. If you feel she is making up complaints just to have the time with you, tell her that you think she doesn't need a Complaints Time any more—and substitute "Tammy's Time" when you can play a game, read a story, chat, or share another positive or neutral activity. Reinstitute Complaints Time when you feel it is appropriate.

You will probably find that the need for a Complaints Time is very minimal; children think it's silly, and probably so do you. It does, however, accomplish three major things:

(a) it lets your child know that there is a time when you will just listen; sometimes this is all he wants;
(b) it teaches him that there is a time and a place for parents to drop everything to listen—and he will learn to wait for that time and place; and

(c) it allows *you* to know that you do not always have to drop everything to listen, especially when most children have a knack of wanting to talk as soon as you are on an important phone call, or on your way out the door, or when they think they can squeeze in another few minutes at bedtime.

Like any other tool, it loses its effectiveness if it is overused and becomes rusty if it is left alone.

*Now, how about some time for yourself?*

# 9

# A Special Note for Management

Even though one of the main points of this book has been to try to help you to organize what you already do and what you want to do, you may have reached this point feeling quite exhausted! Parenting frequently seems like such an overwhelming responsibility, with so many things to think about and to accomplish—and with such a lot riding on it. We have few, if any, immediate ways of telling whether or not we are doing a good job, or whether the decisions we are making are going to pay off in the long run. It is important for us to remember that one of the best ways to teach our children is to model what we want them to do—and at the same time to realize that this is a mixed blessing, since we often try hard to avoid being like *our* parents. We need to learn to turn off the volume and watch the picture if we are ever going to find the encouragement and energy to keep going. In other words, we don't always have to wait until our children acknowledge or like what we are doing or until they verbally agree with us; we can keep a keen eye open for the very small steps that start the longest journeys. We need to feel good about ourselves and who we are, to "get a life" away from family responsibilities; and to allow ourselves to put parenting into the perspective of self as a "whole" individual.

## Delegating

The old truism that has now become almost a cliché is that "it takes a village to raise a child." In these days when families are often isolated from extended family and where big cities have overwhelmed the village, it is often felt by parents that we have to do all the work of raising children by ourselves, increasingly without even a partner. Where some of the work *can* be delegated, it is more frequently to strangers or organizations, rather than to family members or friends with some connection, commitment or loyalty to the parents or children. Parents often feel guilty for delegating childcare responsibilities, with working mothers still viewed from many quarters as somehow abdicating the job of parent, and with stay-at-home fathers having to defend themselves in the face of skepticism and sexism.

It is a fact that the ***ultimate*** responsibility for ***parenting*** our children simply cannot be delegated. There is NO ONE else out there who can or will—indeed, no one who should—do the job as architect of the transition from helpless newborn to competent adult. Once that sperm meets that egg, we're stuck for LIFE. We are, indeed, the "peoplemakers."

Sometimes, parents are unable or unwilling to make this commitment, often because they have not yet had the time or opportunity to "graduate" from trainee to manager. Fortunately for some managers and trainees, adoption frequently matches up both parties—those parents willing to make the commitment and assume responsibility for the children, and those children who did not have a choice in being available.

Regardless of how the trainees arrived in the family company, there is still a normal and natural need to delegate some of the responsibilities of training them to become fully functioning independent adults. For example, we have an overwhelming tendency to delegate the bulk of our children's formal education to the school system, although I must say I sometimes have had occasion to wonder whether parents and teachers realize that this is a delegated responsibility that works best cooperatively. Whether or not early childcare should be delegated is always a topic of controversy. How this should be accomplished is often a topic of even greater controversy. The fact is that many children grow up successfully DESPITE what we do. As psychologist/anthropologist, Dr. Mary Pipher, has so aptly said in her book *The Shelter of Each Other*:

*Children who are ignored sometimes become as strong, beautiful and resilient as sunflowers and sometimes they turn into dangerous psychopaths. Well-meaning families sometimes have extraordinarily bad luck with children, while slapdash parents may raise highly successful children.*

Looking at the family as a small company puts a slightly different perspective on delegation. "Contracting out" or "outsourcing" has become very much a part of what many organizations do when it is recognized that things can be done more efficiently elsewhere by others who possess appropriate skills. In the business world, getting the job done in the most cost-effective way is usually the bottom line—with consumers dictating the minimum limits of quality that will ensure sales. Many families choose to value quality over cost-effectiveness, depending on their policies for the company. Others may well settle for cost-effectiveness, given minimal assurances of quality. Yet others have no concern for quality, just survival. There may be debates both within and outside family units regarding the quality of training provided, and regarding the various priorities that must be shuffled in order to determine the best ways of budgeting the family income.

As we have seen in so many other circumstances, there is no right or wrong here, just different.

## Recharging Batteries

Parenting takes inordinate amounts of energy, even when you feel you don't have any. Many of us run on reserve much of the time. It is critical for each of us to have sources of energy so that we can replenish our levels when low or empty. It may take some effort, but it is worth putting some time in to collecting a list of individuals or activities that serve to fill up the tank, rather than to drain it. Parents are often amazed (and sometimes horrified) at the amount of energy that can be drained by a baby that fits in the crook of your arm, let alone a totally obnoxious, demanding 12-year-old.

It is pretty standard practice in most stress-management programs to teach you to isolate those people and things in your life that drain energy, and to teach ways of saying "no." Some will even go so far as to tell you to cut off all contact with those whose energy flow is in one direction only—out of you, into them. When that "energy drain" is one or more of your children, this becomes something of an impossibility. Thus, it may be worth putting in a little time to think about what you can possibly do to enable yourself to end up with a net ENERGY GAIN, without the need to take more drastic measures. Some options may be found in the list following:

listening to certain music

having a hot bath

being with a friend

having a tall gin and tonic (watch that this is only on occasion!)

talking on the phone

spending time with your partner alone

making love

spending time alone

sitting out under the stars

swimming

walking or jogging

talking to the dog

vegging

thinking

talking with *your* Mom or Dad

reading a book

working

working out

writing poetry

sketching

chopping wood

playing with the kids

playing a sport

punching a punching bag

reciting affirmations

partying

sleeping

*…feel free to add your own*

_____

_____

_____

**Then run through the list when you're feeling depleted.**

## Affirmations for Management

In the absence of management support groups and in the privacy of our own homes, we sometimes need to remind ourselves of some of the basic truths of life as a means of gaining back some energy. Practise saying any or all of these phrases in the mirror to yourself. You will eventually come to believe them.

*I am the best mother/father my children will ever have.*

*I make good choices and decisions, given the information I have at the time.*

*Without discomfort, there is no change. Without change, there is no discomfort.*

*If I don't have to be right, there doesn't have to be conflict. (Thanks, Louise Felton Tracy!)*

*Conflict is normal, natural and necessary.*

*Life is not fair.*

*Parenting is a job, not a mission.*

*To work efficiently, we need to know when to take breaks.*

*This, too, shall pass.*

*No one can make you feel inferior without your permission. (Thanks, Eleanor Roosevelt!)*

*When life throws you a knife, there are two ways to catch it—by the blade or by the handle. (Thanks, Kristie!)*

*Don't sweat the small stuff.*

*Lord, grant me the courage to change the things I can change, the serenity to accept the things I cannot change, and the wisdom to know the difference. (Serenity Prayer)*

## Useful Management Phrases

Over the years, I have had the privilege of listening to hundreds of parents, and I continue to collect various phrases that have been useful to one or many of them. You may have your own that you have found useful and would like to add—or even share with me if you care to! Here is a selection.

*I'm the Mommy, that's why.*

*I'm the Daddy ,that's why.*

*I yell because I care.*

*Who said life was fair?*

*Is there some part of the word NO that you don't understand?*

*If you want an answer now, it's no.*

*Thanks for letting us know.*

*We'll get back to you on that one.*

*Thank you for …*

*I am sorry that I overreacted.*

*What I wanted to get across to you was …*

*When you …, I feel…because…*

*I don't like it when you…I would prefer it if …*

*You're absolutely right!*

*That's not the issue.*

*But I'm not everyone else's parent.*

*Good for you.*

*That's nice.*

*Whatever.*

*Yes, actually, I AM the boss of you.*

*It says so in Chapter One of this book!*

*Tough.*

*Because I said so.*

*That's your decision. That's your choice.*

*I really appreciate it when …*

*I am angry because …*

*I know you can …*

*I love you.*

*When's the last time I told you you're very special?*

# Troubleshooting Using the Family Management Model

The Family Management model can be extremely helpful in terms of trying to figure out where things are going wrong in situations where there is high conflict, or an unusual behaviour, or uncomfortable family dynamics, or trouble upholding a particular expectation, among others. There is a fairly simple process that can be followed in order to try to pinpoint the problem so that steps can be taken to put the management structure in place to try to get the company running smoothly again. While it is a very useful model in a therapy situation, it can also be easily used as a self-help tool for families to do their own troubleshooting.

It is important to remind you at this point that this is not meant to be a substitute for assessment or treatment by a counsellor, psychologist or other mental health professional, or physician. It is a guide to enable you to locate potential problem areas—and decide what you want to do. I am always saddened when people refuse to seek outside help until a major crisis point is reached, and wish very much that the stigma attached to this reaching-out would just go away. I am equally saddened when I hear of professionals who give their clients the impression that they have been doing something wrong, although I recognize that this is what some people seem to hear, even in the middle of being validated. Reassurance and affirmation from a third party—be it a friend or a professional—can be heartwarming and energizing.

When you start your trouble shooting, it is important to try to work through the model from Step 1 to the end. If you try to deal with procedures without looking first at structure, styles or policies, you may find you run into trouble. When you DO run into trouble, back up and see if you have missed something earlier.

## Step 1: Pinpoint the problem.

Start by trying to outline the problem as best you can. Write it down, if that will help. Start asking yourself questions.

What is happening that is causing conflict?

What would I like to change?

How will I know when things are changing?

Who are the main players?

Who else gets involved?

Whose problems IS it? Am I worrying about it more than the other person(s)?

## Step 2: Examine the OVERALL STRUCTURE of the family.

What *is* the structure of the family?

Is it clear to everyone who is who?

Is the management team in place? If not, what is happening to management? Can it be fixed?

Who *is* in charge?

Is this the person/people who *should* be in charge?

Is this the way we want it to be?

Are the trainees working for more than one company?

Does each child have a different role in each company?

Are there cracks in the structure? Is management dealing with these cracks?

Are both managers (if there are two) committed to the same company?

Is management committed to the trainees?

Is the management team sharing the responsibilities in a way that is satisfactory to both parties?

Do both managers have a part to play in parenting the children?

## Step 3:  Evaluate MANAGEMENT STYLES

Do we, as individuals and as managers, have different styles?

What are they?

What is my own preferred style? Does it change from child to child?

What other factors can cause it to change? Am I in control of these factors?

Am I an extravert or an introvert?

Is my partner an extravert or an introvert?

To what degree are the differences between us causing problems?

To what degree are the differences between us helpful in providing a fuller range of skills and talents?

Do differences in style affect other aspects of our relationship? Which ones?

Does something need to be done about this? Do we need help with this?

What are the general personalities of our trainees and how do they blend with ours?

How do our trainees' personalities blend with each other?

Are we aware of how our different trainees affect our management style?

Are we aware of how our management style affects our different trainees?

Am I trying to convince my partner that my style of management is better? (Of course, I know it *is*!)

Is my partner trying to convince me that his or her style of management is better?

Can we try recognizing that "different" is not "wrong"?

Can we see ways in which our unique individual styles can be useful in certain situations?

## Step 4: Discuss Company POLICIES

Is there a policy in place to cover the issue we are concerned about?

What is it?

Do we understand where this policy came from?

Do both managers subscribe to the same policy?

Are we comfortable with the policy?

Is it a policy or a procedure? Are we talking about a general philosophy or a specific rule?

Can it be worded "In this family we…," in which case it's a policy?

If there is no general policy in place, can we find one that management can live with?

Do we know in our own minds why we have this policy in place?

Have we communicated the policy clearly to the children?

Do they understand it? Can they say it in their own words?

What message does this policy convey?

Is it a message we want family members to get?

## Step 5:  Establish Procedures to Go With the Policies

Is the issue negotiable or non-negotiable?

Does management agree on this?

If it is non-negotiable, is it clear that there is no choice?

Are there negotiable components to the issue? Are these separated out from the non-negotiable parts?

If there are choices, are these stated positively?

Can management live with all of the choices offered? If not, work on this until we can.

Is the consequence of each choice clearly explained?

Is the consequence a natural, logical or arbitrary one?

If it is an order, is it stated as such—or could it be misinterpreted as a request or advice?

If I'm sounding a bit authoritarian, can it be softened by making it a request? Will my child still comply?

Am I able and willing to follow through with the consequences I have promised?

Are the trainees receiving any reinforcement for making choices?

Are we expecting children to *like* the various choices they have?

Am I spending a lot of time trying to make them like them?

Are we reinforcing the behaviour we want from our children?

Am I giving them mixed messages by expecting one thing and accepting another?

Am I making the choices for them because it is easier than watching them do it?

## Step 6: Monitor Progress

Am I watching the picture to see the small but positive changes, or am I waiting for perfection?

Do I recognize that things may get worse before they get better?

Can we weather the inevitable challenges to the new order?

Am I working on my daily affirmations?

Do I have a life?

Have I done a sense-of-humour check and tune-up?

Do we need an objective opinion as to how things are going?

Can we use each other for that?

If not, do I have an "inner circle" of consultants—friends or family members?

If not, do I know someone I could ask for advice? Family physician? A minister, rabbi or priest? A family counsellor? An employee assistance program?

Have I thought about reading this book again, especially the parts I skipped the first time?

Am I out of energy?

## Step 7:  Reward myself!

Choose to do something(s) on my Recharging Batteries list.

## A Final Word

Sometimes we might be under the impression that parenting is a serious business. One saving grace that can help us through the most difficult times is to maintain a sense of humour. Children can be hysterically funny in their attempts at growing up, and *we* can paint a pretty humorous picture as we try to pretend we know what we're doing. Seeing the funny side can sometimes be quite difficult, and sometimes not appropriate, but whenever it's possible, humour can turn a mountain back into the molehill that it probably is. As my own Mum would have said: "If you didn't laugh, you'd cry."

To end on an appropriate note, I shall quote my favourite saying from one of the greatest humorists of all time, Mark Twain, who said of his adolescence:

*When I was a boy of fourteen, my father was so ignorant I could hardly stand to have the old man around. But when I got to be twenty-one, I was astonished at how much he had learned in seven years.*

However young or old your trainees may be, may you managers have fun managing, learning and *living*.

**Dr. Maggie Mamen** is a clinical psychologist in private practice, who specializes in working with children, adolescents and their families. She gives frequent workshops and seminars for community groups, teachers and parents of children of all ages, and has taught university courses on child development and exceptional children since 1981. Born in London, England, Maggie came to Canada in 1971 with her then-boyfriend, now-husband of 25 years, Rolf, and discovered as a perk that she could take a course for free while she worked as a secretary at Carleton University. After tossing a coin to decide whether that course would be sociology of psychology, she eventually decided that she had found her niche, and enrolled in a B.A. program. Over the following years, Maggie and Rolf welcomed three "trainees," daughters Natalie and Katy and son Jorin. Maggie became adept at studying for exams and "writing" papers in her head as she was playing with toddlers, doing laundry and changing diapers. She admits that her youngest child's first phrase was "Mommy busy." After earning her Ph.D., Maggie worked as a psychologist for both a hospital and a school board before deciding that she was intrinsically more of a manager than a trainee, and branched out into her own practice in Nepean, Ontario. She has never looked back.

# Bibliography

Some of these books have been mentioned already; others are added for interest. This is not meant to be an exhaustive list, but rather a taste of what is out there.

**Coloroso, Barbara:** *Kids Are Worth It!*, **Somerville House, Toronto, 1994**
    A warm, practical approach to different parenting styles and ways to get the family working.

**Dinkmeyer, Don and McKay, Gary:** *Parenting Teenagers: Systematic Training for Effective Parenting of Teens,* **American Guidance Services, Circle Pines, Minnesota, 1990**
    This is just one of the series of STEP program books that cover all ages from babies right up to teens. It is full of excellent suggestions for communicating with teens and consequenting different behaviours. Just make sure the issue IS negotiable before entering some of the verbal debates!

**Dodson, Fitzhugh:** *How to Discipline With Love,* **Penguin Signet Books, New York, 1978**
    A broad range of ideas about how to provide your children with structure and consequences; and some tips on how to hold family meetings; special chapters on single parenting, step-parenting and different age levels.

**Faber, Adele and Mazlish, Elaine:** *How To Talk So Kids Will Listen and Listen So Kids Will Talk,* **Avon Books, New York, 1980**
    One of the best books on communicating with children.

**Faber, Adele and Mazlish, Elaine:** *Siblings Without Rivalry,* **Norton, New York, 1987**
    Some fantastic insights and suggestions on how to deal with conflicts among your children.

**Fraiberg, Selma:** *The Magic Years,* **Distican, Richmond Hill, Ontario, 1966**
    A wonderful look at the world of infants and young children from inside the mind of the child; excellent view of behavioural and moral development.

**Fisher, Roger, Ury, William and Patton, Bruce:** *Getting To Yes: Negotiating Agreement Without Giving In,* **(Second Edition), Penguin Books, New York, 1991**
    This book written for businesses, unions and management to assist with negotiating disputes "without getting taken—and without getting angry"—many parallels to running the family company.

**Gray, John:** *Men Are From Mars, Women Are From Venus,* **Harper Perennial, New York, 1992**
    A look at the vast differences in perception between males and females and how they lead to misunderstanding and miscommunication.

**Hendrix, Harville:** *Getting the Love You Want,* **Henry Holt, New York, 1988, and** *Keeping the Love You Get,* **Pocket Books, New York, 1992**
    Guides for partners who want to examine and improve the management team.

**Lawrence, Gordon:** *People Types and Tiger Stripes* **Third Edition, Centre for Applications of Psychological Type Inc., Gainsville, Florida, 1996**
    A great book to introduce you to Myers-Briggs personality "types" and how they interact, including sections on children's learning styles and other issues with school. Good insights into how the different "types" work together (or not!) in groups.

**Lerner, Harriet Goldhor:** *The Dance of Anger,* **Harper and Row, New York, 1985**
    A "must read" for partners who want to stay with the company but make some changes from within.

**Marshall, Peter:** *Now I Know Why Tigers Eat Their Young,* **Whitecap Books, Toronto, 1992**
    Lots of good suggestions in the context of raising teenagers and surviving.

**Marshall, Peter:** *Cinderella Revisited,* **Whitecap Books, Toronto, 1993**
    A look at step-parenting and blended families, written with humour and down-to-earth advice.

**Neumann-Clubb, Angela:** *Love in the Blended Family: Falling in Love with a Package Deal,* **NC Press Ltd., Toronto, 1988**
    Yet another look at step-parenting and blended families—this time focusing more on the emotional aspects.

**Phelan, Thomas W.:** *1-2-3 Magic*; Child Management Inc., Glen Ellyn, Illinois, 1995
    A superbly practical guide to training your children to do what you want—ages 2 to 12.

**Pipher, Mary:** *Reviving Ophelia: Saving the Selves of Adolescent Girls,* **Ballantine Books, New York, 1994**
    Simply the best book I have ever read on understanding adolescent girls—I only wish there were a similar one for boys.

**Pipher, Mary:** *The Shelter of Each Other: Rebuilding Families,* **Grossett-Putman Books, New York, 1996**
An intriguing and encouraging look at families from a number of different perspectives, with some messages about the potentially dangerous influences of the media and the information explosion.

**Sark:** *Inspiration Sandwich: Stories to inspire our creative freedom;* **Celestial Arts, Berkeley, California, 1992**
A laid-back, whimsical, creative book full of quirky affirmations—just for fun.

**Satir, Virginia:** *Peoplemaking,* **Science and Behavioural Books Inc., Palo Alto, California, 1972**
One of the classics for professional family therapists, parents and anyone else who is interested in family dynamics—full of inspiration and insights.

**Schmidt, Fran, and Friedman, Alice:** *Fighting Fair for Families,* **Peace Education Foundation, Miami, Florida, 1990**
An excellent, brief, easy-to-read book with large cartoon pictures chock full of hints on preventing the escalation of conflict by recognizing common "fouls" and developing new communication patterns.

**Tannen, Deborah:** *You Just Don't Understand!,* **Ballantine Books, New York, 1990**
Various ways in which males and females communicate differently —and the roots of misunderstandings.

**Tracey, Louise Felton:** *Grounded for Life?!,* **Parenting Press Inc., Seattle, Washington, 1994**
The subtitle of this book says it all: "Stop blowing your fuse and start communication with your teenager."

**Visher, Emily B., and Visher, John S.:** *How to Win as a Step Family,* **Second Edition, Brunner/Mazel, New York, 1991.**
Some insights into the roles of individuals in the step family context, and some suggestions as to how to make things work.

**Von Couver, Maria:** *Don't Say No, Just Let Go,* **Pulp Press Book Publishers, Vancouver, BC, 1991**
A tongue-in-cheek view of managing older trainees—and easing the transition out of the nest. Written by a group of individuals with wonderful humour and some solid common-sense suggestions.

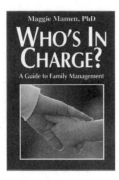

To order additional copies of
## Who's in Charge?
**A Guide to Family Management**

ISBN 0-921165-47-1   $21.95 CAN  $18.95 US

Contact Creative Bound Inc. by phone at **1-800-287-8610** or by e-mail at orderdesk@creativebound.com. Ask about our discounts for wholesale, retail, library, educational, association and multiple-copy orders.

# Additional resources by Dr. Maggie Mamen

### Laughter, Love & Limits: Parenting for Life
ISBN 0-921165-54-4
Trade paper, 6 x 9
208 pages
$24.95 CAN  $21.95 US

With warmth, wisdom and wit, Maggie Mamen explores the various myths associated with parenting, and creates a general parenting philosophy with three main goals:

#3   Loving children enough to set reasonable limits until they can set limits of their own

#2   Giving ourselves, as parents, permission to be leaders in the family

#1   Showing our children there is hope for the future.

### The Pampered Child Syndrome:
How to Recognize It, How to Manage It and How to Avoid It.

ISBN 1-894439-16-3
Trade paper, 6 x 9
160 pages
$24.95 CAN  $20.95 US

This book provides insight and support for parents, teachers and other professionals who are trying to deal with pampered children, and who can thus be constructive influences in promoting change by working together as a team. The goal is for parents to take back the power they have given away, and to be confident in raising resilient, empathic and mentally healthy children who are well-prepared for the world outside the family.

### Nonverbal Learning Disabilities and Their Clinical Subtypes: Assessment, Diagnosis and Management*
ISBN 0-9688279-0-X
Spiral bound, 5.5 x 8.5, 100 pages
$12.00 CAN  $10.00 US

This handbook is for parents, teachers and other professionals who live or work with individuals with nonverbal learning disabilities. Four different subtypes of NLD are described (perceptual, social, written expressive and attentional), along with a wide range of remedial and compensatory strategies that are useful both at home and at school.

*Also available in French edition: *Les Troubles D'Apprentissage Non Verbaux et Leurs Sous-Types Cliniques: Evaluation, diagnostic et gestion*